THE
BONDAGE
BREAKER®
THE
NEXT STEP

NEIL T. ANDERSON

HARVEST HOUSE PUBLISHERS

EUGENE, OREGON

THE BONDAGE BREAKER®—THE NEXT STEP
Copyright © 1991/2011 by Neil T. Anderson
Published by Harvest House Publishers
Eugene, Oregon 97402
www.harvesthousepublishers.com
Library of Congress Cataloging-in-Publication Data
　Anderson, Neil T.
　The bondage breaker—the next step / Neil T. Anderson.
　　p. cm.
　ISBN 978-0-7369-2954-7 (pbk.)
　1. Christian life. 2. Suffering—Religious aspects—Christianity. 3. Sex crimes—Religious aspects—Christianity. 4. Compulsive behavior—Religious aspects—Christianity. 5. Counseling—Religious aspects—Christianity. I. Title.
　BV4909.A53 2011
　248.8'6—dc22
　　　　　　　　　　　　　　　　　　　　　　　　　　　　　2010031625

Acknowledgments

I have a lot to be thankful for. I had a good childhood. Being raised on a farm taught me many lasting values that I cherish to this day. Education was never stressed by my parents, but all five siblings have graduate and postgraduate degrees and love the Lord. I have a good marriage. Joanne has been a faithful companion with a sincere devotion to God. My children have remained in the faith and teach their children to do likewise. The Freedom in Christ Ministry staff members around the world are more than colleagues. They are my friends, and we enjoy working together. Harvest House has been a great publisher for me and a partner in ministry. Finally, God loves me, and He loves you. Life is good. Thank You, Jesus!

For years I have told others that the good you see in me is Christ. I take no credit for that. We are what we are by the grace of God. Other than Christ, the good you see in me is my mother. She could have risen to the top in any profession she chose, but she chose to be a servant. She had many reasons to complain, but she never did. Her mother died when she was eight years old. The family became dysfunctional, and she wed my father to escape a bad situation. She became a farmer's wife and learned the trade well. Under her guidance, we never missed Sunday school or failed to do our lessons. She always worked behind the scene and was the force that held everything together. The bank where she worked gave her a special position because of her rapport with the public. After retirement she volunteered with hospice and called on seniors until she was 85 years old herself. All her children are serving others. What a legacy.

She died a year before this book was printed, and I dedicate it to her memory. This world became a better place wherever Bertha Anderson served. I always wanted to be like her when I grew up. Thanks, Mom.

CONTENTS

INTRODUCTION

When I graduated from seminary, I looked forward to being the captain of the Gospel Ship. I would sail off into eternity and rescue a few people from the watery abyss. We would have Bible classes, clubs for the kiddies, and sports for the athletically inclined (for the purpose of outreach, of course). Everybody would learn to love one another.

Off I sailed on my first pastoral assignment, but it wasn't long before I noticed a dark ship sailing alongside. On that ship were people struggling with alcohol and drug addiction, anxiety disorders, anger, depression, sexual bondages, and abuse of every conceivable kind. One day I realized that I was on the wrong ship. God had called me to serve on the dark ship, but not to be the captain because He is the Skipper. Through a series of life-transforming events, I changed ships—only to discover they were two images of the same ship!

Our churches are filled with hurting people. Many wear masks, hoping others won't see their inner turmoil. They cling to whatever hope they can and long for the acceptance, affirmation, and freedom that Jesus offers to every one of His children.

This book is about resolving personal and spiritual conflicts through genuine repentance and faith in God. The process, which I call Discipleship Counseling, incorporates and depends on the presence of Christ.[1] He is the only One who can bind up the brokenhearted and set the captives free. You will read actual accounts of courageous people who have agreed to tell their stories from their perspective. Some have been called into full-time ministry. Their names, occupations, and geographical references have been changed to protect their privacy. Each testimony has been chosen specially to teach biblical principles that I hope will equip the church so that as people become free, they can help others. I pray this book will help you in your own journey.

I have added my comments and instruction, but you will learn a lot from the stories. People readily share what they have suffered, but their testimonies go way beyond that. They share their inner struggles and expose the battles raging in their minds. That alone is worth the price of the book.

The integrity of the church is at stake. We are all in this mess because of the fall, and the only answer is to establish God's children alive and free in Christ. God has given us the ministry of reconciliation, which is the process of removing the barriers to our intimacy with God. That cannot happen without genuine repentance and faith in God, and He is the One who grants those things (2 Timothy 2:24-26). When I seek to help another person, there are not just two parties present. God is always present, and only He can bind up the brokenhearted and set a captive free. If I try to play God in another person's life, it won't work. God is the One who convicts us of sin, grants repentance, and leads us into the truth, which sets us free. Nor can I assume the responsibility of the other person. Knowing who is responsible for what is invaluable if we want to live balanced lives and be effective in ministry.[2]

Hope for the Hopeless

A pastor friend asked if I could find some time to help his wife. I empathized with him because counseling one's own spouse is not advisable. This woman is a wonderful lady, and people see her as competent and composed, but she struggles inwardly on a daily basis. (I don't counsel or disciple the opposite gender for more than one or two sessions, and I also advise others not to do so.) I heard her story and asked if she would like to resolve those issues. That is a question I always ask, and nobody has ever said no. We set up an appointment, and I led her through the Steps to Freedom in Christ.[3] A week later I received this account in a letter from her:

How can I say thanks? The Lord allowed me to spend time with you just when I was concluding that there was no hope for me to ever break free from the downward spiral of continual defeat, depression, and guilt. I did not know my identity in Christ or recognize the enemy's accusations.

I grew up in church and have been a pastor's wife for 25 years, so everyone thought I was as put together on the inside as I was on the outside. On the contrary, I had no infrastructure on the inside and often wondered when the weight of trying to hold myself together would cause my life to fall apart and come crumbling down. It seemed as if sheer determination was the only thing that kept me going.

When I left your office last Thursday, it was a beautiful, crystal-clear day with snow visible on the mountains, and I felt as if a film had been lifted from my eyes. The CD player in my car was playing a piano arrangement of "It Is Well with My Soul." The words of the song fairly exploded in my mind with the realization that it was well in my soul... for the first time in years.

The next day at work, when people asked me, "How are you today?" I immediately responded, "I'm doing great! How about you?" In the past I would have mumbled something about being almost alive. One person replied, "Boy, something must have happened to you yesterday!"

I have heard the same songs and read the same Bible verses as before, but it is as if they're totally new. Now I'm experiencing joy and peace in the midst of the same circumstances that used to bring defeat and discouragement. For the first time, I have wanted to read my Bible and pray. It is hard to contain myself—I want to shout from the rooftops what has taken place in my life, but my real desire is for my life itself to do the shouting.

Already the deceiver has tried to plant thoughts in my mind that this won't last, that it's just another gimmick that won't work. The difference is that now I know those are lies from Satan and not the truth. What a difference freedom in Christ makes!

What a difference indeed! Is there anything special about me that made this encounter with God so effective? Do I have some unique gift from God or special anointing? No, I don't think so. People all over the world are using the same message and method I use with similar results because we believe that God is the Wonderful Counselor, the Great Physician, and the only One who can bring about such change.

Several exploratory studies have shown promising results regarding the effectiveness of Discipleship Counseling. Judith King, a Christian therapist, did three pilot studies in 1996. The participants had attended a conference called Living Free in Christ, where they were led through the Steps to Freedom in Christ.

In the first study, 30 participants took a 10-item questionnaire before completing the Steps. The questionnaire was re-administered three months after the conference. The questionnaire assessed levels of depression, anxiety, inner conflict, tormenting thoughts, and addictive behaviors. The second study involved 55 participants who took a 12-item questionnaire before completing the Steps and then again three months later. The third pilot study involved 21 participants who also took a 12-item questionnaire before receiving the Steps and then again three months afterward. The following table illustrates the percentage of improvement for each category.

	Depression	Anxiety	Inner Conflict	Tormenting Thoughts	Addictive Behavior
Study 1	64%	58%	63%	82%	52%
Study 2	47%	44%	51%	58%	43%
Study 3	52%	47%	48%	57%	39%

The Living Free in Christ conference is now available as a curriculum entitled *Freedom in Christ Small Group Bible Study* (Gospel Light, 2008). It has a leader's guide with all the messages written out and a learner's guide for each participant (which includes the Steps to Freedom in Christ). It also includes a DVD of me delivering 12 messages so leaders can choose between showing the DVD to the group or presenting the messages themselves. The content of the course is the core message of Freedom in Christ Ministries and is developed in my first two books, *Victory over the Darkness* (Regal, 2000) and *The Bondage Breaker* (Harvest House, 2007).

Research was also conducted in Oklahoma City, Oklahoma, and Tyler, Texas, by Dr. George Hurst, former director of the University of Texas Health Center at Tyler, Texas. The Oklahoma and Texas data were combined into a manuscript that was accepted for publication by the *Southern Medical Journal*, the official journal of the Southern Medical Association. The study completed in Texas was in cooperation with a doctoral student at Regent University under the supervision of Dr. Fernando Garzon, who presently teaches at Liberty University.

Most people attending a Living Free in Christ conference can work through the repentance process on their own using the Steps to Freedom in Christ. In our experience, about 15 percent can't because of difficulties they have experienced. A personal session with a trained encourager was offered to them. They were given a questionnaire before a Steps to Freedom in Christ session and again three months later with the following results given in percentage of improvement:

	Oklahoma City	Tyler
Depression	44%	52%
Anxiety	45%	44%
Fear	48%	49%
Anger	36%	55%
Tormenting thoughts	51%	27%
Negative habits	· 48%	43%
Sense of self-worth	52%	40%

How Does It Work?

In January 2000, I taught a doctor of ministry class at Regent University. Dr. Fernando Garzon, who taught in the department of psychology at the time, requested permission to conduct research on the students who attended. The class was a one-week intensive session, meeting eight hours every day. The students were working on their master of divinity, doctor of psychology, and doctor of ministry degrees. Dr. Garzon used Judith King's questionnaire. In addition, the students took a pretest and posttest using the Rosenberg Self-Esteem Inventory, the Beck Anxiety Inventory, and the Symptom Checklist 90-R. Dr. Garzon's results were published in the *Journal of Psychology and Theology*. He included this note in his summary:

> Statistically significant reductions were found in several scales of the SCL-90-R (global severity index, anxiety, depression, obsessive-compulsive, interpersonal sensitivity, hostility, somatization, paranoid ideation, and psychoticism). Anxiety was reduced as measured by the Beck Anxiety Inventory, and

statistically significant increases in self-esteem and spirituality items were also found.

Of course, most students at that level of education don't expect a class
to change their lives, but that is exactly what happened. Most students
enroll in classes like these to fulfill degree requirements and gain some
skills for ministry. Nor does such a class represent the general population.
These were all committed Christians taking graduate-level classes.

How does one explain such significant results? I can assure you that
the results we are seeing routinely in our ministry have little to do with
our personal counseling skills. In fact, no professional counselors or pastors participated in the research I've described. The encouragers were all
trained lay ministers. The editors of the *Journal of Psychology and Theology* asked an appropriate question: "How does Neil explain such results?
What is he doing beyond cognitive therapy?" In other words, are these
classes and conferences simply applying cognitive therapy to groups? My
response is that cognitive therapy is part of the process, but cognitive therapy alone cannot fully explain the results.

From a Christian perspective, cognitive therapy is similar to the biblical
concept of repentance, which literally means "a change of mind." People
do what they do and feel what they feel because of what they believe or
think. Therefore, they need to change the way they think or believe. That
is the basic theory of cognitive therapy. The therapeutic process could be
summarized like this:

1. The therapist shows the client the connection between negative
   thoughts and beliefs, the emotions they create, and the behavior that follows.

2. Then the therapist teaches the client to notice when he is having
   negative thoughts or a distorted view of reality. If thoughts or
   beliefs lead to negative feelings and improper responses to life,
   the client learns to identify them as ineffective or dysfunctional.

3. Next, the client examines the evidence for and against such distorted thinking or perceptions of reality. What does the evidence
   indicate? Is the client going to continue to think in this way, to
   believe those thoughts, and to act accordingly, or will the client change what he believes and thinks? Now it is decision time.

4. If the client concludes that what he has believed is not true and that his perception of reality is not accurate, then he must learn to substitute new ways of thinking, believing, and responding.

5. Finally, the client learns to identify and change the inappropriate assumptions that predisposed him to distort the experience in the first place.

Beyond Cognitive Therapy

While doing research for the book *Freedom from Fear*, I read Dr. Edmund Bourne's book *Healing Fear* (New Harbinger, 1998). Dr. Bourne wrote an earlier book entitled *The Anxiety and Phobia Workbook* (New Harbinger, 1995), which won the Benjamin Franklin Book Award for Excellence in Psychology. After writing that first book, Dr. Bourne went through the worst period of anxiety he had ever experienced. It caused him to reevaluate his own life and approach to treatment. In the foreword to the later book, Dr. Bourne describes the change.

The guiding metaphor for this book is "healing" as an approach to overcoming anxiety, in contrast to "applied technology." I feel it's important to introduce this perspective into the field of anxiety treatment since the vast majority of self-help books available (including my first book) utilize the applied technology approach. These books represent—in a variety of ways—the mainstream cognitive behavior methodology for treating anxiety disorders. Cognitive behavior therapy reflects the dominant zeitgeist of Western society— a worldview that has primary faith in scientifically validated technologies that give humans knowledge and power to overcome obstacles to successful adaptation...

I don't want to diminish the importance of cognitive behavior therapy (CBT) and the applied technology approach. Such an approach produces effective results in many cases, and I use it in my professional practice every day. In the past few years, though, I feel that the cognitive behavioral strategy has reached its limits. CBT and medication can produce results quickly and are very compatible with the brief therapy, managed-care environment in the mental health profession at present.

When follow-up is done over one to three year intervals, however, some of the gains are lost. Relapses occur rather often, and people seem to get themselves back into the same difficulties that precipitated the original anxiety disorder.[4]

I don't want to diminish the important contribution of cognitive behavioral therapy (CBT) either, but I believe that CBT by itself is not enough for three reasons. First, even as Christians, if we use the words of Christ without the life of Christ, we will not see the kind of results mentioned previously and achieve the resolution that Scripture indicates. Truth is far more than words from the Bible. Jesus is the truth, and He is the One who sets us free. When we are born again, we share His eternal life.

Encouraging people to believe the truth as an intellectual maneuver may bring about some changes in mood and behavior, but words by themselves cannot change who we are. We need the life of Christ for that. Adam and Eve were created to be spiritually alive, which means their souls were in union with God. They died spiritually when they sinned. Jesus came to give us life. The early church understood salvation to mean union with God. Christianity is not an intellectual exercise—it is a relationship with our heavenly Father.

Second, Discipleship Counseling is primarily an encounter with God as opposed to applied technology or the application of counseling techniques. God knows every intimate detail of the people I try to help. He knows exactly what their problems and needs are, and He alone is the answer. The Holy Spirit will lead all God's children to the truth that will set them free if we include Him in the process.

Third, CBT will not be as effective as it could be if the encourager doesn't take into account the reality of the spiritual world. "The Spirit clearly says that in later times some will abandon the faith and follow deceiving spirits and things taught by demons" (1 Timothy 4:1 NIV). That is presently happening all over the world. The apostle Paul also wrote, "I am afraid that just as Eve was deceived by the serpent's cunning, your minds may somehow be led astray from your sincere and pure devotion to Christ" (2 Corinthians 11:3 NIV). Such scriptural passages and years of experience have helped us to understand the spiritual battle for our minds.

The secular world refers to these deceptions as chemical imbalances, but how can a chemical produce a personal thought? Or how can our neurotransmitters randomly create thoughts that we are opposed to thinking? Those who are defeated by condemning, accusing, tempting, and blasphemous thoughts should ask themselves a simple question: *Did I want to think that thought? Did I consciously choose to think that?* For your sake, please pay special attention to the stories in this book as they describe the battle for the mind. The church would be revolutionized if Christians fully understood this simple truth.

Antipsychotic drugs may temporarily silence anguished thoughts, but they don't cure anything. Many people drink alcohol and take drugs to drown out those thoughts. They get a temporary reprieve from the mental assault, but they wake up in the morning a little worse than before. Scripture admonishes us to take every thought captive to the obedience of Christ (2 Corinthians 10:5), to actively put on the armor of God (Ephesians 6:10-17), and to choose to think about things that are true, noble, and right (Philippians 4:8).

This book is somewhat of a sequel to my first two books, *Victory over the Darkness* and *The Bondage Breaker*. This book will show the practicality of the message and method they describe. You will learn a lot by hearing from these people, and I hope my notes and explanations will greatly enhance your personal growth and ability to help others. The apostle John explained how victorious Christians win the battle: "They overcame [Satan] because of the blood of the Lamb and because of the word of their testimony" (Revelation 12:11).

The Bondage Breaker was my second doctoral dissertation. I had several objectives for my second doctoral degree.

1. I wanted to find a biblically balanced answer for the problems people have.

2. I wanted the answer to be holistic from a purely Christian perspective. The Bible does not present theology, psychology, pneumatology, and physiology as separate, unrelated entities. God deals with us as whole people, He takes all reality into account, and He does so all the time. (I may be the only pastor who has coauthored with Christian therapists, doctors, theologians, and missionaries, and who has written books on depression, anxiety disorder, anger, chemical addiction, sexual addiction, marriage, parenting, and leadership.)

3. The message and method had to be true for all people at all times.

4. The method of Discipleship Counseling had to include God and to maintain control—that is, to prevent Satan from manifesting himself. Most counselors and many pastors will probably never choose to get involved in a ministry where demons are manifested. In training for Discipleship Counseling, encouragers learn how to maintain control and to stop any manifestations of the enemy. God does everything decently and in order.

5. The process had to include both inner healing and deliverance. Various denominations and other Christian movements emphasize some aspects of healing and recovery, but usually not all. Discipleship Counseling is a discipling and counseling process that leads to both inner healing and deliverance. For some those are four different and even distinct ministries. For me they are all the same. Dr. Bourne shares that conviction:

> In my own experience, spirituality has been important, and I believe it will come to play an increasingly important role in psychology of the future. Holistic medicine, with its interest in meditation, prayer, and the role of spiritual healing in recovery from serious illness, has become a mainstream movement in the nineties. I believe there will be a "holistic psychology" in the not too distant future, like holistic medicine, [which] integrated scientifically based treatment approaches with alternative, more spiritually based modalities.[5]

I hope Dr. Bourne is right, and I pray that this book will illustrate my conviction that he is. In the last three chapters you will hear from two Hispanic pastors, an African-American pastor, and Rich Miller, who is president of Freedom in Christ Ministries in the United States. They will share their stories and vision for this ministry. Jesus came to set captives free and bind up the brokenhearted. Let me share with you how I believe He does that. You may even be motivated to participate in this ministry of reconciliation.

FREEDOM FROM THE CYCLE OF ABUSE

I have started seminars with this question: "In the short time that I am here, if I really got to know you, would I like you? I mean, really got to know you intimately?"

I once asked a seminary class that question, and a student responded, "You'd feel sorry for me!" It was said in jest, but it captured the perspective of many who live in emotional isolation. Lost in their loneliness and pain, they cling to a thin ray of hope that somehow God will break through their fog of despair.

Here is my answer to that question: I think I would, but not because of any great qualities you or I may have. God has taken up residence in me, and He reaches out to everyone who has been abused. The system has not been kind to them. The parents who were supposed to provide the nurturing love and acceptance they needed were, instead, the cause of their plight. The church they clung to for hope didn't seem to have the answers they were looking for.

Such is the case of our first testimony. I had never met Molly before I received a rather lengthy letter sharing her newly found freedom in Christ. Months later I had the privilege to meet her. I expected to see a broken-down, dumpy human being. Instead, the person who had lunch with my wife and me was a professional, intelligent, and attractive woman.

You will form your own mental picture as you hear her story. I did not personally provide counseling for Molly. She found her freedom by watching the Freedom in Christ course on video in Sunday school. She is the product of a dysfunctional family and an inept church. Millions of people who are living in bondage would joyfully step into freedom if their churches showed them who they are in Christ and helped them resolve their personal and spiritual conflicts.

> My whole life has changed since I attended the Freedom in Christ course. The source of my lifelong bondages became clear to me for the first time. I am 40 years old, and I feel that I have just reached the promised land.
>
> I was born in a rural community in grassroots USA to two of the meanest people I have ever met. My father was a farmer with very little education who married my mother at a young age. He was one of 15 children in a family plagued by mental illness. My mother's family is unstable as well, but they deny there is a problem.
>
> The bright spot among my relatives was my grandmother. I'm sure that without her, I would have gone over the edge long ago. She was a saint, and I knew she loved me.
>
> I was the firstborn, but my parents had been married for 12 years when I was born. In my first memory of them together, my mom locked my dad outside at night. I can still see the fierce expression on his face as he looked at me through the door and yelled, "Molly! Open the door and let me in!"
>
> My mom, who was standing directly behind me, screamed, "Don't you dare open that door!"
>
> One evening, as my mother and father were getting ready to go out, my one-year-old sister and I were in their bed, probably waiting for a babysitter. Suddenly I saw an evil appearance, exactly like the classic red devil, dancing at the end of the bed. I was petrified and felt compelled not to tell anyone exactly what I was seeing.
>
> I called my mother, crying as I told her only that something was in the room. She replied, "There's nothing here." I pulled up the covers so I couldn't see the end of the bed as she turned out the light and left the room. I stayed under the bedcovers for a long time, afraid to look out. When I did, the presence was still there, laughing.
>
> My mother and father divorced when I was four. Later, I remember the two of them meeting on the street, stopping to chat, and my

daddy asking my mother if he could have my sister. Those words felt like a knife going through my heart because they meant that my father did not want me.

The voices probably started then: *Your father doesn't even want you.* And it was true. He told me all through my life that I was just like my mother. I knew what that meant because he hated her. She was a rageaholic, and her outbursts of anger terrorized me.

When I was about six, I was at my dad's house, and an aunt said to him, "Molly looks like you." Instantly, his whole demeanor changed, and he stood up and screamed at her, "She looks exactly like her mother! I lived with that woman for sixteen years, and she looks like her mother!" With that, he stomped out of the house, and I felt a sharp pain shoot through my chest.

Members of our family thought my mother might harm us. Once when my mother was really bad, an aunt came to our home and stood outside one of our windows. She was watching over us because she worried about our safety. Mother cursed us a lot of the time and totally controlled our lives. She had no friends, no love or tenderness, and she often said her life would have been a lot better without me. She resented us, and we were a bother to her.

In the next couple of years, Mom became even more bitter and mean. For the remainder of my years with her, I feared for my life. Though I didn't know much about the spiritual world, I felt even then that Satan was involved in our home.

A time came when I would not eat my food unless my mother ate hers first because I was so afraid she would poison us. I can't describe the terror of being a child who always lived with a foreboding threat of danger. Though some of our relatives feared for us as well, they feared her more, so they never did anything about it.

When I was 14, my mother decided that I'd lost something, and she refused to listen when I tried to tell her that I never had it. She beat and cursed me from six in the evening until one in the morning, making me go from room to room. I even had to go outside in the dark and rummage through the trash, searching over and over again for the item. I guess she finally got tired and went to bed. I was looking for the top to the toothpaste tube!

After that incident, we went to our monthly visit with our dad. He probably would have seen us more, but his new wife ranted and raved the whole time we were with them. She treated us much the same way our mother did. On the way home, my mind suddenly blanked out. I could not remember who I was or who all the people in the car were. A huge lump welled up in my throat, and I was so scared, I couldn't talk. Then, just as suddenly, when Dad turned onto our street, my memory came flooding back. Oh, how I hated walking back into my hellish home, but there was nowhere else to go.

Through all of this, I desperately wanted the love of my father and mother. All the way into my thirties, I called my mom every day even though she would often slam the phone in my ear. I was still trying to get her to love me.

When I was quite young, one of my uncles, who had a number of children of his own, occasionally came over to our house and took me out. Apparently, it never occurred to my mother to be cautious and question why he would do that. From the time I was four until I was seven, he fondled me and threatened to tell my mother that I was smoking cigarettes if I told her what he did. I remember feeling tremendous guilt, thinking I should have said no, but I was too afraid to.

After that I became addicted to masturbation, a problem that I never could control until I found my freedom in Christ. That sexual desire has tried to come back, but now I know what to do about it. I just proclaim aloud who I am as a child of God and tell Satan and his evil cohorts to leave me. The compulsion leaves immediately.

Recently, I decided to tell someone about that sexual addiction so I would be accountable. I chose one of my friends from a Bible study, and she said, "I've always had that problem too." We cried together, and I told her of my victory over that demonic influence and all the violent sexual thoughts that went along with it. I rejoice now that I no longer have to be subject to the evil presence associated with that act and its overwhelming power. In Christ, I am free to choose not to sin in that way.

Life got even worse as I grew older. I don't remember when, but I started to pray that God would not let me lose my mind and end up in an institution. I knew that could happen very easily because I had been hearing voices as long as I could remember. I had seen movies like *The Three Faces of Eve*, in which people lost touch with reality, and I could see how that could happen to me.

We had no spiritual life. My mother totally rejected Christianity and wouldn't let me talk about it with her. My dad went to church every Sunday but was extremely legalistic—a trap I later fell into. I began attending a neighborhood church as a teenager and became very legalistic, doing *everything* they told me to do to make sure I would be happy when I was older.

At the age of 14, I asked Jesus Christ to be my Savior, and I was thrilled. I couldn't wait to learn all I could about Him. The first time I went to a youth group, they distributed some books and gave us an assignment to do. By the next week, I had answered all the questions and purchased a notebook. Someone saw that I had completed the work and yelled out, "Look, everybody, she even answered the questions." The whole group laughed, and I never did another assignment.

Sunday school was worse. A lot of girls in our church were wealthy, and everyone in our Sunday school class was in a sorority except me and one other girl. We would call each other every Sunday morning to be sure we would both be there because the others didn't talk to us, and neither of us wanted to be there alone.

All during this time I was plagued by terrible thoughts. *You're ugly. You're disgusting. You're unworthy. God couldn't possibly love you.* My life seemed to have a way of making me believe that about myself.

The oppression, depression, and condemning voices continued, but no one knew. I had no one to talk to. I thought I was getting what I deserved. When I tried to tell people what my mother was like, they either didn't understand or responded inappropriately. Once I confided in a Sunday school teacher, and she said, "Let's go talk to your mother." That struck icy fear in my heart because I knew what I would get from my mother after the teacher left, so I wouldn't do it. I was too terrified.

I lived by a code of self-effort, trying to please my mother to keep her from becoming angry. I believed that God put me where I was, and if I could stand suffering, be obedient, and live a good life and not sin, He would let me find happiness when I got married. My goal was to have a Christian home and a Christian husband so I could find happiness and a secure place where no one would abuse me.

The summer after my senior year I met a man I had seen at our high school graduation, and it was love at first sight. He was the man I would marry for happiness ten months later, when I was 19. We were in church every Sunday and every Wednesday night, and we went to everything else there was to attend. But we had no friends and were never invited to anyone's home.

Our church didn't offer premarital counseling, and marriage was a big shock. I had saved myself for marriage, but I hated sex. Within a week, my husband began straying away, sometimes for a weekend. We moved into an apartment, and with the boxes still unpacked he simply left to play golf and be with his friends.

That was the final straw after a lifetime of never having felt loved by anyone. My self-esteem was so low that when I realized my husband didn't care anymore, I just went to bed and sank into a deep depression. Three weeks later, I felt convicted and got up. I thought, *How could he love me? He couldn't respect someone who clung to him and tried to hold on for dear life to his every move.* So I tried to change and make our marriage work. Somehow, we managed to stay together for 15 years of conflict, rejection, and pain. We vacillated between living a legalistic pretense of Christianity and completely turning our backs on God.

I hoped having a child would bring happiness, and when I couldn't get pregnant, I started seeing doctors. When my 50-year-old doctor was kind and held my hand, I felt he was just being fatherly. But then he fondled me while I was on the examination table. Later, when I developed a lump in my breast, I went to another doctor, and he did something similar.

I wasn't the kind of person who was flirty; I could hardly look another person in the eye. I believe that is just the way Satan works, using others to bring evil into our lives when we are vulnerable. I felt so uncomfortable while these things were happening, but being uncomfortable was normal for me. Later, one of my friends who worked in a law firm called and told me that one of those doctors had done the same thing to someone else and was being sued. That's when I finally knew that it wasn't me, and I was relieved of some of the doubts about myself. My thought processes were so wrong that I just didn't know what was right.

I finally got pregnant and was catapulted into motherhood. Not very long after that, my husband came home one night and said, "All the guys at work talk about girls and sex, so I spend most of my time with Linda. She goes to our church and is a Christian, and I go on breaks with her." He asked if I minded, and I said I didn't.

My friends had warned me that he was seeing other women, but I wouldn't believe it. I just said, "He wouldn't do that." That was my way of dealing with it because I wanted to avoid the pain of finding out that he was unfaithful. Eventually he left me for Linda.

When my husband walked out and left me with two babies, I gave up on God and blamed Him for all the pain. I learned in church that the way to happiness for a single girl was to marry a Christian, and I had done that. Now I was angry at God, and for six years I ignored Him.

My mother urged me, "Do something. Don't just sit there with your life. Do *something* even if it is wrong."

The people from work wanted me to go to the bar with them, and though I had never been to a bar, I went and soon got into that life-style. I had never intended to date seamy people, but the lowest class of people made me feel better. I even went to bars where some of the people had no teeth! I guess that was the only place I felt okay about myself because they were worse off than I was.

I was still bound by legalism and sometimes would try to go to church, but it took a herculean effort. On Friday evenings I would go to the bar, and when my kids came home from visiting their father on Saturday, I would go back to being a good little mother. On Sunday I would try to take them to church, but when I did, I felt like a nail was being driven into my temple. I had always had a lot of headaches, but this pain was excruciating. Sometimes I would get sick and have to leave, and once I threw up in the car, so I finally quit going to church.

I remember one of the last sermons I heard. The preacher said, "There is a downward spiral. When it starts, the circle is really big and things are moving slowly at the top. As it goes down, things get closer and closer together and go faster and faster until they are out of control. But you can prevent the downward spiral by not taking that first step."

I had already taken that first step. Things did get out of control, and I couldn't stop. When I got depressed, I would go to the bar and someone would say something nice to me. I would have a drink, and temporarily I didn't feel so bad. I found plenty of acceptance at the bar but very little at church. I had been in church regularly since I was 14, but I never had a close friend. I was so withdrawn and people didn't seem to reach out, so I just sat there, miserable and alone.

I was in such a bad place in my life. In the bars, people got into knife fights and sometimes pulled a gun. But as time passed, I sunk to the place where I would even go and drink by myself and ignore the danger. I really didn't care anymore what happened.

I had a brush with cancer, which frightened me, so I thought maybe God was stomping on me to get my attention. So I quit the bars and went back to church. But after a year I forgot my cancer scare and slipped back into my old lifestyle. I was living such a lie that it was inevitable. I had always had a strong conscience before, but at that time I remember thinking, *I don't even feel bad about this.*

I was miserable and thought of suicide, but I was such a chicken I couldn't do it. My life was so out of control that when I met a man at the bar who wanted to marry me, I rushed headlong into it. I didn't ask God what He thought about it because I knew what His answer would be, and I didn't care. The guy was still married when I first met him and was a client where I worked. I was so afraid he would mention that he knew me from the bar—I wanted to keep that part of my life secret. I married him out of desperation to find happiness, but we were only together for two years.

Even before that marriage, I had slipped back into a legalistic cycle in which I tried to control everything. We went to church, and I made sure my husband read everything I wanted him to read. But he was more sick than I was and very weak, with no sense of his own identity. In the beginning, I could control everything. But when his two daughters came to live with us, all hell broke loose. Their mother had been in a mental hospital and was now living in a lesbian relationship. The girls were totally without discipline, and I decided I was going to save them, but my efforts blew up in my face.

I asked my husband to leave because I knew he was planning to leave me anyway, and I wanted to get the jump on him. I filed for divorce, but then I couldn't sleep at night, and I stopped the proceedings. I knew it was wrong. I told him that he could get a divorce if he wanted to, but I never heard from him again.

My second husband and I did go for counseling, but no one was able to help us. They didn't acknowledge the reality of the spiritual world, so how could they help us? They just patted us on the hand and said everything would be all right.

Finally, my last counselor did acknowledge that I was in a spiritual battle. I told him repeatedly about my fear of dying, my thoughts of suicide, my inability to feel loved by God, my cloud of despair that overwhelmed me when I came home...but he didn't seem to know how to help me.

He asked me if I loved God, and I said, "I don't know." He responded, "Well, I know you do." I told him that the only God I knew was up in heaven with a hammer waiting to beat me. He argued with me that God was not like that, but it didn't help.

I didn't tell him about the big black spider I saw as I woke up in the mornings. It's incredible while it is happening. I convinced myself I was having a nightmare with my eyes wide open.

I got to the point where I couldn't stand pretending anymore. I would cry all weekend and pray, "God, I can't pretend anymore that I'm okay." I would get up when the kids came home from their weekend and put on my good-mother act. The truth was that all weekend I lay on the couch in utter blackness. I didn't open the windows and never went out. I never talked to anybody because of the voices in my head: *They don't want to talk with you. They don't like you.* I never realized that I was paying attention to deceiving spirits.

I would do okay at work, but the second I walked in the door at night, a cloud was waiting there to engulf me. I would usually just lay on the couch again, feeling miserable. Menial things like going to the grocery store were really difficult because I thought all the people there hated me.

I kept going to the last counselor because I was desperate and couldn't keep up the pretense any longer. I was even crying at work. I told my counselor, "I'm losing my mind. I'm miserable. I can't go on."

He gave me a book to read, but it never got to the core of the problem. Although it spoke of Christ, there was no resolution; there was only hope if you could go to one of their clinics it described. However, the book did refer to malignant codependency, and I knew that was me: no friends, totally isolated, living a lie, not knowing who I was. That terrified me.

After I read the book, I went to my counselor and said, "This is me."

I was on the verge of suicide, but he simply told me to come back in two weeks. I tried to get into the clinic but couldn't because I didn't have the money they required.

My sister was also going through serious problems at the time, but she couldn't go to the counselor at our church because she wasn't a member. They were so overloaded they couldn't take nonmembers. My counselor recommended a class for children of dysfunctional families at another church. I wanted to go too, but it was hard to start over with a new group of people.

When the weekend came, my children went away, and I spent all Friday night and all day Saturday on the couch, totally depressed and eating nothing but popcorn. By Sunday the thought came that I should attend the class. Nothing in the world could have been harder to do, but somehow I gathered the courage to go. I attended regularly and it helped a lot. It was so good to have friends even though they were sick themselves.

One of my new friends invited me to a different class where they were showing a video series by Neil. As I watched the video, my mouth fell open and I found myself saying repeatedly, "This is the truth." After the first visit, I wouldn't have missed that class for anything. Once I even went when I was sick because nothing in my life had given me such hope.

When I heard Neil talk about people hearing voices, I was so excited because I'd finally found someone who knew what I was experiencing. Then he talked about Zechariah 3, where Satan accuses the high priest and the Lord says, "I rebuke you, Satan." That truth set me free. I thought, *I can do that.*

I realized I had been deceived by the father of lies. He had been accusing me all my life, and I had never stood against him. I learned that because I am alive in Christ and seated with Him in heaven, I have authority to resist deceiving spirits and reject Satan's lies. I left that evening floating on air.

The depression is gone, the voices are gone…even the huge spider-like object I have been seeing in my room for the past ten years when I wake up is gone!

My employer gave me the Resolving Personal and Spiritual Conflicts audio series (based on Neil's first two books, *Victory over the*

Darkness and *The Bondage Breaker*) for Christmas, and I have been listening to them over and over again. There's light in my mind where there was darkness before. I love the light now and open the curtains and windows to let it shine in. I really am a new person! I have people into my home for a Bible study with the CDs, something I couldn't have done before.

As I look back over my life, I see that the messages I got from my family were all negative. I can't remember really feeling love in my life until I saw the video series and realized that God loves me just as I am.

Before I found my freedom in Christ, I was behaving just as my mother had, going into rages with my kids and then hating myself afterward. That is so rare now, and my children feel comfortable with me.

I'm not like I was; I'm being healed. When I see myself falling back into old habits or thought patterns, I know what to do. I don't have to grovel in self-pity. At each point of conflict I can recognize the lies and deception and then stand against them by deliberately choosing what I now know to be true.

My goal is to be the kind of parent God wants me to be, and I believe He will make up for all the years the locusts have eaten (Joel 2:24-25).

How People Live

Nobody can consistently behave in a way that is inconsistent with what they believe about themselves. Molly believed that she wasn't any good, that nobody wanted her, that she wasn't worthy of love. She was living a distorted life, foisted on her by abused and abusive parents. The cycle of abuse would have continued on to her children if the grace of God had not intervened. People will remain products of their past unless they are given opportunities to become new creations in Christ.

When I hear a story like this—and I hear a lot of them—I just pray that people like Molly could be hugged by someone in a healthy way for every time they have been touched wrongly. As a parent I want to apologize to her for the poor parenting she received. As a professional man I want to ask her forgiveness for the way men have raped her and touched her inappropriately. That was not her fault; it was due to the sickness of men who see women as sex objects instead of children of God who are created in His image.

Stopping the Abusive Cycle

As believers, we have the power we need to live productive lives, and we have the authority we need to resist the devil. People like Molly are not the problem, they are victims—victimized by the god of this world, by abusive parents, by a cruel society, and by legalistic churches.

How do we stop this cycle of abuse? We lead people to Christ and help them establish their identity as children of God. We teach them the reality of the spiritual world, and encourage them to walk by faith in the power of the Holy Spirit. We provide them an opportunity to resolve their personal and spiritual conflicts through genuine repentance and faith in God. We do that by becoming the pastors, parents, and friends God wants us to be. We share Jesus' compassion for those who suffer: "It is not those who are healthy who need a physician, but those who are sick. But go and learn what this means, 'I desire compassion, and not sacrifice,' for I did not come to call the righteous, but sinners" (Matthew 9:12-13).

The Path Back to God

I am not advocating a quick fix for difficult problems. Processing the Steps to Freedom in Christ can take hours, and that is not the end. In fact, it only affords a new beginning toward maturity in Christ. Growth cannot occur until the conflicts are resolved. You can't mature in Christ if you believe a pack of lies about yourself and God. You can't grow if you are holding on to bitterness and won't forgive as Christ has forgiven you. You are not going to make progress in your journey if you are prideful, because God opposes the proud. The message to the church is, repent and believe. A failure to do so only leaves us in bondage to sin.

Helping people to recognize deception and counterfeit guidance and to choose the truth isn't simple. Getting them in touch with their emotional pain and helping them forgive their abusers isn't easy. Helping them overcome their problems of pride, rebellion, and sin requires godly love and acceptance.

Many people are able to process the Steps to Freedom in Christ on their own as Molly did because Christ is the Wonderful Counselor. However, many others need the assistance of godly encouragers who understand the grace of God and have the knowledge of His ways. Discipleship Counseling relies on the presence of God and the leading of the Holy Spirit.

We are suffering from a paralysis of analysis. A perfect diagnosis of the problem does not provide the answer. If I were lost in a maze, I wouldn't want someone to explain to me all the intricacies of mazes and then give me coping skills so I can survive in the maze. I certainly wouldn't need a legalistic Christian scolding me for getting in the maze in the first place. I would desire and desperately need clear directions out of there. People don't like living in bondage, especially when they don't have to. God sent His Son as our Savior, provided the Scriptures as a road map, and sent the Holy Spirit to guide us. People all over the world are dying in a lifeless maze for want of someone to gently show them the way, the truth, and the life.

2

MAINTAINING FREEDOM THROUGH STAGES OF GROWTH

God's will for our lives is for our sanctification (1 Thessalonians 4:3). As believers, we are in the process of conforming to His image. Every pastor and Christian counselor who is working with God should be contributing to that process. Many people are not growing because they lack the knowledge they need. Others are not even able to receive the truth because of unresolved conflicts in their lives (1 Corinthians 3:1-3). That was the case for Anne. Before we get to her story, let's consider the sanctification process.

The apostle Paul wrote, "As for you, you were dead in your transgressions and sins, in which you used to live when you followed the ways of this world and of the ruler of the kingdom of the air, the spirit who is now at work in those who are disobedient" (Ephesians 2:1-2 NIV). Every descendent of Adam is born into this world physically alive but spiritually dead (that is, separated from God). During our early and formative years, we learned how to live our lives independent of God. We had neither the presence of God in our lives nor the knowledge of His ways.

This learned independence from God is characteristic of the flesh, or old nature. The flesh develops defense mechanisms that enable us to cope, succeed, and survive without God. Defense mechanisms are conceptually similar to what some call mental strongholds or flesh patterns.

Eternal life is not something we get when we physically die. We are spiritually alive the moment we are born again. That means that our souls are in union with God. As the apostle Paul commonly writes, we are "in Christ" or "in the Beloved" or "in Him." The apostle John says, "The testimony is this, that God has given us eternal life, and this life is in His Son. He who has the Son has the life; he who does not have the Son of God does not have the life" (1 John 5:11-12). What Adam and Eve lost in the fall was life, and life is what Jesus came to give us (John 10:10).

We need the life of God to grow because nothing grows without life. At the moment of our conversion, all of God's resources became available to us. However, our minds were not instantly reprogrammed. Until God's transformation process begins, our minds are still conformed to the world and regimented by it. The apostle Paul writes, "Do not conform any longer to the pattern of this world, but be transformed by the renewing of your mind. Then you will be able to test and approve what God's will is— his good, pleasing and perfect will" (Romans 12:2 NIV).

Therefore, the task of Christian education is to disciple God's children, who have been previously programmed to live independently of God, to begin living a life that depends on Him. This requires genuine repentance and a renewing of the mind, which cannot happen apart from Christ, who indwells us. We need the life of Christ in order to change. Many people never come to Christ or fail to grow because they don't want to acknowledge Jesus as Lord. They want to be captains of their souls and masters of their fates. Self-rule requires self-sufficiency, and that leads to defeat. "Not that we are adequate in ourselves to consider anything as coming from ourselves, but our adequacy is from God, who made us adequate as servants of a new covenant, not of the letter [of the law] but of the Spirit, for the letter kills, but the Spirit gives life" (2 Corinthians 3:5-6).

And if the task of Christian education is to disciple God's children, the task of Discipleship Counseling is to free believers from their past by connecting them to the source of life. They have to be firmly rooted in Christ in order to grow in Him (Colossians 2:6-7). Discipleship Counseling establishes believers alive and free in Christ so they can mature in Christ. Old defense mechanisms aren't needed anymore because Christ is our defense.

Being Transformed

Truth and obedience are key to living a Christ-dependent life. However, we can believe the truth only if we understand it, and we can obey commands only if we know them. As the Holy Spirit leads us into all truth, we must respond by trusting and obeying. "The one who says, 'I have come to know Him,' and does not keep His commandments, is a liar, and the truth is not in him" (1 John 2:4). We give Satan an opportunity when we fail to believe the truth and act in disobedience. According to Ephesians 2:2 (NIV), that spirit "is now at work in those who are disobedient."

The process of sanctification begins at our new birth and ends in glorification. In the New Testament, sanctification is presented in the past, present, and future tenses. We have been sanctified, we are being sanctified, and someday we shall be fully sanctified. Past-tense sanctification is often referred to as *positional sanctification*, and present-tense sanctification is referred to as *progressive sanctification*.

Positional sanctification refers to what has already been accomplished by Christ, which the believer has received by faith. It refers to our position in Christ as children of God. As born-again believers, we are not trying to become children of God; we are children of God who are becoming like Christ. "But as many as received Him, to them He gave the right to become children of God" (John 1:12). This is important to understand because all the defeated Christians I have worked with didn't know who they were in Christ, nor did they understand what it meant to be a child of God. Our identity and position in Christ are the basis for our growth in Christ.

Defusing the Past

In many cases, traumatic experiences in the past continue to have debilitating effects today. But Christians are not in bondage to past traumas. Rather, they are in bondage to the lies they have believed as a result of the abuses. In the previous chapter, Molly believed a lot of lies about herself because of her abusive parents. Many of these experiences are commonly blocked from memory. Psychologists are aware of this and often attempt to bring hidden memories to light through psychotherapy, hypnosis, and drug therapy. Their sincerity is commendable, but I cannot endorse any procedure that doesn't include God in the process.

You will find no instruction in Scripture to dwell on yourself, direct your thoughts inward, or encourage a passive state of mind through hypnosis or other means. Instead, we can follow David's helpful example and invite God to search our hearts (Psalm 139:23-24). Occult practices encourage a passive state of mind, and Eastern religions admonish us to bypass the mind altogether. God never bypasses our minds. He works through them for our transformation (Romans 12:2).

This is especially true when we see manifestations of the Spirit, and it is the way we distinguish between the true gifts of God and the counterfeit. The mind is not engaged when exercising counterfeit spirituality. In the context of discussing the gifts of prophecy and tongues, which are spiritual manifestations, the apostle Paul's instructions are pertinent: "What is the outcome then? I will pray with the spirit and I will pray with the mind also; I will sing with the spirit and I will sing with the mind also" (1 Corinthians 14:15). "Brethren, do not be children in your thinking; yet in evil be infants, but in your thinking be mature" (verse 20).

If our thoughts, emotions, and actions suffer because of hidden memories, God will wait until we are mature enough for Him to reveal them to us. The apostle Paul refers to this process in 1 Corinthians 4:3-5 (NIV):

> I care very little if I am judged by you or by any human court; indeed, I do not even judge myself. My conscience is clear, but that does not make me innocent. It is the Lord who judges me. Therefore judge nothing before the appointed time; wait until the Lord comes. He will bring to light what is hidden in darkness and will expose the motives of men's hearts. At that time each will receive his praise from God.

This passage clearly indicates that God knows things about us that we ourselves do not know. We will never know ourselves perfectly in this lifetime. We frequently encounter people who can't recall periods of time in their lives. Some will mentally dissociate during times of extreme abuse. This allows these people to develop somewhat normally. Like any defense mechanism, it breaks down over time and is no longer necessary after we have come to Christ. That is why some people start to recall early childhood traumas later in life.

Pursuing God

What should we do if we suspect something in our past has never been resolved and is still affecting us, but we don't know what it is? We should continue to pursue God, discover who we are in Christ, and learn how to walk by faith in the power of the Holy Spirit. In other words, rather than trying to find out what is wrong about you, begin discovering what is right about you as a new creation in Christ. As we become more secure in Christ, He reveals more to us about who we really are. As we become more aware that He is the only defense we need, He starts to wean us from our old mechanisms for defending ourselves. In other words, we should solidify the answer, which will empower us to resolve problems as they surface.

Stripping off old defense mechanisms and revealing character deficiencies is like peeling layers off an onion. When one layer is removed, we may feel great and think we are done. We feel the same way the apostle Paul did—we have nothing against ourselves and are free from what others think of us, but we have not yet fully arrived. At the right time, God reveals more of our deficiencies in order to share in His holiness.

Our next story is about this progressive sanctification. Anne wrote the following account halfway through a conference. She learned who she was in Christ, how to walk by faith, and how mental strongholds affect the battle for her mind. She was so excited that she couldn't wait to go through the Steps to Freedom in Christ in class. She went home and processed the Steps on her own.

> Praise God, I think this is the answer I've been searching for. I'm not crazy! I don't have an overactive imagination as I have been told and believed for years. I'm just normal like everybody else.
>
> I have struggled through my whole Christian experience with bizarre thoughts that were so embarrassing that I rarely told anyone else about them. How could I admit to someone in the church what had crossed my mind? I tried to honestly talk with a Christian group about some of the things I was struggling with. People sucked in their breath, there was a still silence, and then someone changed the subject. I could have died. I learned quickly that these things are not suitable topics for discussion in the church, or at least they weren't at that time.
>
> I didn't know what it meant to take every thought captive. I tried to do this once, but I was unsuccessful because I blamed myself for all this stuff. I thought all those thoughts were mine and that I was the one who was creating them. A terrible cloud had always hung over my head because of these issues. I never felt righteous, so I couldn't accept the fact that I really was.

Praise God, it was only Satan—not me. I have worth! The problem is so easy to deal with now that I know what it is.

I was abused as a child. My mother lied to me a lot, and Satan used the things she said, such as "You're lazy. You'll never amount to anything." Over and over he has fed me so much junk and preyed on my worst fears. At night I would have nightmares that the lies were true, and in the morning I would be so depressed. I have had a difficult time shaking this stuff.

Being abused, I was taught not to think for myself. I did what I was told and never questioned anything for fear of being beaten. This set me up for Satan's mind games. I was conditioned to have someone lie to me about myself, primarily my mother. I feared taking control of my mind because I didn't know what would happen. I believed I would lose my identity because I wouldn't have anyone to tell me what to do.

In actuality, I have gained my identity for the first time. I am not a product of my mother's lies, and I am not a product of the garbage Satan feeds me. Now I'm finally me, a child of God! Through all this junk, Satan has terrorized me. I have been living in fear of myself, but praise God, I think that time is over. I used to worry whether a thought came from Satan or myself. Now I realize that's not the issue. I just need to examine the thought according to the Word of God and then choose the truth.

I feel a little unsure writing this so soon. Maybe I should take a "wait and see" attitude, but I am sensing such joy and peace that I feel in my gut it must be real. Praise God for the truth and answered prayer! I am free!

One layer of the onion was exposed, and the problem was corrected. Anne discovered who she really is in Christ. She is no longer a product of her past abuses. She is a new creation in Christ. With that foundation laid, she was able to identify the lies she had believed and choose the truth. When she tried to share some of her struggles in the past, she was rejected, probably because others in the group were struggling in a similar fashion but were unable or unwilling to reciprocate.

I long for the day when our churches will help people get firmly rooted in Christ and provide an atmosphere where people like Anne can share the real nature of their struggles. Satan does everything in the dark. God does everything in the light. When issues like this arise, let's not suck in our breath and change the subject. We play into Satan's schemes by keeping everything hidden. Let's walk in the light and have fellowship with one another in order that the blood of Jesus will cleanse us from all sin (1 John 1:7). God is light, and in Him there is no darkness at all (verse 5). We need to lay aside falsehood and speak the truth in love, for we are members of one another (Ephesians 4:15,25).

Now Anne knows who she is, and she understands the nature of the battle going on for her mind. So now she is totally free, right? Positionally yes, but not progressively. She dealt with what she knew, but God wasn't through with her yet. One layer doesn't constitute the whole onion. Two weeks after the class she wrote another report.

> Good night! Where do I start? Let me say that I attended the class for academic reasons. I could not have fathomed in advance what the Lord had in store for me. In fact, I probably wouldn't have believed it anyway. I guess I should start where I left off a few days ago.
>
> I explained that I had been freed from obsessive thoughts. A few months ago, I had specifically asked the Lord to help me understand this problem. When I heard the information in the class at the beginning of the week, I was thrilled. It was exactly what I had asked the Lord for. At home I prayed through all of the prayers in the Steps to Freedom in Christ. It was a struggle, but the voices stopped. I felt free, and I thought I was done. Little did I know!
>
> Neil talked to me one evening after the session and told me that I probably needed to forgive my mother. I wasn't so sure because I had tried to forgive her once before, and it didn't work. I now realize that I was pushed into it by some well-meaning Christians who said that my feelings didn't matter. In fact, they said I shouldn't even have any angry feelings. So I grudgingly went through the motions of saying that I forgave the people who hurt me. As a result of that phony effort, I became very bitter and sarcastic. I tried not to be, but the truth is that I was. God showed me later that I actually became even more bitter because I denied that I was angry while going through the motions of forgiving.
>
> A year ago I attended a support group for abuse victims. The leader of the group told me that I was bitter because I had tried to forgive

before I was ready. She said that I needed to work through all my feelings about each incident. After that, I would be able to forgive.

When Neil talked to me, I thought he was coercing me into another ritual prayer of forgiveness that would mean nothing. All I knew was that I couldn't return to the bitterness trail. I decided to just take the information that I received at the beginning of the class as what God wanted me to receive and put the rest of the information on the academic shelf.

Thursday evening, when Neil spoke on forgiveness, I was miserable. I had a horrible time sitting through the meeting, feeling bored and angry. I felt very misunderstood and thought I was wasting my time. I knew I couldn't leave without making everyone think I was possessed or something. So I struggled with staying awake and couldn't wait to get out of there.

That night I started working on an assignment for a class. I couldn't process anything because the forgiveness issue hit me square in the face again. I felt angry, but something in my gut told me that there had to be something more to what Neil was saying. I decided that I should be open and willing to try anything. I figured it couldn't hurt, although I really doubted that it would help since I had been trying to forgive my parents for years.

So I made a list of people and the offenses and worked through them as Neil had suggested that night. During that time, God showed me that I had been hanging on to their offenses in anger in order to protect myself against further abuse. I didn't know how to scripturally set boundaries around myself for my protection. I was taught that I must keep turning the other cheek and letting others slap it. When Neil spoke of what it really means to honor our parents, I knew that was my ticket to freedom.

God showed me that it was okay to stick up for myself and that I didn't need an unforgiving attitude to protect myself. He showed me that the abuse support group was right in telling me to focus on my emotions; however, there was never any real closure because they never taught us to come to a decision about forgiveness. That was always down the road—when I felt better. But I never felt better. I see now that both Christian groups were emphasizing individual aspects about forgiveness but not integrating them.

After forgiving, I felt exhausted. Interestingly, though, I immediately had a real love jump in my heart for Neil. It hadn't been there before.

I went to sleep feeling pretty good, but before long, I had another one of my awful nightmares. I woke up cold and sweaty, and my heart was racing. I hadn't had a nightmare in several months, so I was kind of surprised. For the first time in my life, it occurred to me that maybe this wasn't all a result of my abuse as I had been taught in the past. I prayed that the Lord would help me figure it all out, and I went back to sleep.

At 2:30, my roommate woke me up with her screaming. I jumped out of bed and woke her up. We compared notes and realized we both had similar dreams. After praying together and renouncing Satan, we went back to bed and both slept fine the rest of the night.

In those early morning hours as I was drifting back to sleep, God showed me that I had been having similar dreams since third grade—dreams that I had met the devil and that he put a curse on me. I can't believe I forgot all that! I asked the Lord what happened in the third grade and remembered that I had started watching *Bewitched* at that time. It was my favorite TV show, and I watched it religiously.

Because of that show, I became very interested in spiritual powers. Along with many of my school friends, I read books on ghosts, ESP, palm reading, and spells and curses. Playing with Magic 8 Balls, Ouija boards, and magic sets was also popular. *Gilligan's Island* was another TV favorite, and watching that, I got the idea to use voodoo dolls to get back at my mother. I considered putting a curse on her. By the time I was in the sixth grade, I was so depressed. I started reading Edgar Allan Poe, and eventually craved his stories. *I can't believe I had forgotten all this!*

In high school the dreams came back, and I became suicidal. By the grace of God, I invited Jesus Christ into my life soon after that. The biggest thing God showed me was that when I was very young, I was aware of evil power and desired to have it.

When Saturday came, I was all ears. This wasn't hocus-pocus to me anymore. As Neil led us through the Steps to Freedom in Christ, I prayed all the prayers again and renounced all the lies that have been going on in my family for years. I acknowledged my own sin and lack of forgiveness.

This is the best way I can describe what happened to me this week: I feel as if I had been in a cult for a long time, but now I have finally been deprogrammed. That's the way it was for me. It was as though God locked me in a room and said, *Give me your brain. We're not leaving here until you do.* It's taken an intensive week to get me to see the lies I have been believing. I had no idea.

Since I have returned home, the lying thoughts—*You're no good, you're stupid,* and *no one likes you*—have been coming out in full force. I told my husband everything, so now when I have a lying thought, I tell him, and we both laugh about it and talk about what's really true. Praise God! I was too embarrassed to tell him before.

Last night one of my nightmares started up again. I felt oppression coming on as I was drifting off to sleep. I said Jesus' name out loud right away, and I could feel the oppression lifting off my heart quickly, almost as if it had been torn away. Praise God!

Because of counseling through the years, I have quite a few notebooks filled with accounts of pain from my past. This pain pile has been sitting in my drawer and has been an eyesore every time I looked at it. I now know that my identity isn't in the past anymore; it's in Christ. I burned all the notebooks.

I'm thankful for this opportunity to hear the truth even though I didn't understand it at first. The joy I feel is the same joy I felt when I first received Christ! Finally, I understand what it means to be a child of God.

Three layers of the onion peeled off in one week is remarkable. Anne understood her identity in Christ, she was able to forgive others from her heart, and she learned to stand against the fiery darts of Satan. She had much more going for her than most struggling Christians. She was receiving Christian instruction and had a loving and supportive husband to go home to. Other people can resolve the same issues with less support, but for some it may take significantly longer.

Forgiveness Brings Freedom

We need to expand on several issues. Every Christian will face the need to forgive others. When people express feelings like anger and bitterness, telling them they shouldn't feel that way is counterproductive. We cannot resolve our feelings without acknowledging them. If we want our emotional wounds to be healed, we have to get in touch with our emotional core. God will surface our emotional pain so we can forgive and be freed from it. We don't heal in order to forgive; we forgive in order to heal.

Forgiveness sets us free from our past. Harboring bitterness against others is like swallowing poison and hoping they will die. To forgive is to set captives free—only to realize that we were the captives! This is the path to gaining our own freedom. We don't forgive others for their sake. We do it for our sake and for the sake of our relationship with God.

"But you don't know how bad they hurt me," says the victim. But that's not the point—they are *still* hurting you, so the real issue is, how do you stop the pain? You stop *your* pain by forgiving *others* from your heart, which means that you acknowledge the hurt and the hate, and then by the grace of God, you let it go. To not forgive from the heart is to give Satan an opportunity (Matthew 18:34-35; 2 Corinthians 2:10-11).

Bringing up the past and reliving all the pain without taking steps to forgive only reinforces the hurt. The more you talk about it, the stronger the hold it has on you. Trying to suppress the truth won't work either—you'll just bury the pain alive. God surfaces the issue so you can forgive and let it go.

Stand Against Sin

Many, like Anne, see their anger as a means of protecting themselves against further abuse. Some secular counselors see Christian forgiveness as codependency, and they urge their clients, "Don't let that person shove you around anymore. Get mad!" Instead, I say, "Don't let that person shove you around anymore. Forgive!"

Then take a stand against sin. Forgiveness does not include tolerating the ways in which others may be sinning against you. God forgives, but He doesn't tolerate sin. I am grieved when I hear Christians advise others to go home and be submissive in abusive relationships with their husbands, parents, and other authority figures. Perhaps these unhelpful counselors should go to the victims' homes and take their abuse for them!

But doesn't the Bible say that wives and children are to be submissive? Yes, it does, but that is not all it says. God has established governing authorities (Romans 13:1-7) to protect abused children and battered wives. Abuse is illegal, and abusers should be reported to governing authorities. In many states the law requires such reporting. My intent is not to be vindictive, but rather to encourage you to confront your abusers for their sakes and, if necessary, to report them to the proper authorities. You never help abusers when you allow them to continue their abuse. Most of them have been abused as well and need help.

If a man in your church abused someone else's wife, would you tolerate that? If a man or woman in your church abused someone else's child, would you tolerate that? Spousal and child abuse are not only wrong, they are double crimes. Family members not only get abused but also lose their protection. Husbands and parents are to protect and provide for their spouses and children. Never are they given license to abuse, nor should abuse ever be tolerated. Report these people's actions for everyone's sake, or the cycle of abuse will continue on to the next generation.

A mother of three children shared in tears that she knew she needed to forgive her mother. But if she forgave her that evening, what was she to do that next Sunday, when her mother expected her and her family to come over for lunch after church? "She will just bad-mouth me all over again."

"Put a stop to it," I said. "When you go to her house next Sunday, say something like this: 'I love and respect you, but you have been bad-mouthing me all my life. It isn't doing you any good, and it certainly isn't doing me any good. For the sake of my husband and children, I can't be a part of that anymore. If you can't stop treating me that way, I am going to stop coming over here.'"

But doesn't the Bible say she is supposed to honor her mother and father? Precisely—letting her mother systematically destroy her and her present family would not be honoring her mother. In the Old Testament, to honor your mother and father primarily means to financially take care of them when they are no longer able to care for themselves. Besides, the admonition to obey one's parents no longer applies to this mother because she was given away in marriage. Her primary responsibility is to her husband and children.

Living with Consequences

We are to forgive as Christ has forgiven us. What has His forgiveness accomplished? He took the sins of the world upon Himself. He suffered the consequences of our sin. When we forgive the sins of others, we are agreeing to live with the consequences of their sin.

But that's not fair! Of course it's not fair, but if we want to be free, we must forgive anyway. We are all living with the consequences of other people's sin, including Adam's sin. But we have a choice: We can deal with those consequences in the bondage of bitterness or in the freedom of forgiveness. For your sake, choose the latter.

Some victims have asked, "Why should I let them off my hook?" That is precisely why you should. If you don't forgive, you are still hooked to them and to your past. Even if you move away from your abuser, and even if your abuser dies, you still need to forgive. When you let others off your hook, are they off God's hook? Never! "Vengeance is mine, I will repay," says the Lord (Hebrews 10:30). God will deal justly with everyone in the final judgment, which is something we cannot do.

Including God in the Process

We must include God in this process. In the Steps to Freedom in Christ, the third step deals with bitterness versus forgiveness, and it begins with a prayer asking God, *Reveal to my mind those people I have not forgiven so that I may do so.* I have heard some people respond to that prayer by saying, "There is no one that I need to forgive." Then I ask them to share names that come to their minds, and out comes a list of people. If we ask, God will get beyond our denial. God will bring to the surface not only names but also memories of painful experiences. He doesn't want us to live in the bondage of bitterness, whereby many are defiled.

For each name that God surfaces, the Steps instruct people to pray, *Lord, I forgive* [name] *for* [name the offenses]. If you are helping people work through the Steps, stay with them until they have acknowledged every painful memory. It is often helpful to have them say, "I forgive [name] for [what they did or didn't do] because it made me feel [rejected, unwanted, dirty, and so on]." This helps them get in touch with their emotional core, which is necessary if they are going to forgive from their heart.

Layers of the Onion

When people finish the Steps and feel free, they may struggle again a few days or weeks later. They may conclude that the process didn't work, but that is probably not true. Like Anne, they could be dealing with new issues that hadn't surfaced before—new layers of the onion. Christians need to resolve the issues they are aware of. If they are unwilling to do that, God knows they are not ready to go to the next level. If they show themselves faithful in little things, God will put them in charge of greater things.

The onion effect is significant for those who have been sexually abused and even more pronounced for those who have been satanically ritually abused. The Lord usually begins with early childhood memories and works forward. We need to help these people get firmly rooted in Christ and then help them resolve past conflicts as God reveals them. As their memories surface, they will usually have something to renounce and someone to forgive.

Being firmly rooted in Christ as a child of God is a prerequisite for growing in Christ. You can observe this by the rapid growth that takes place after conflicts are resolved. However, we are still living in a fallen world, where Satan is the ruler. The need to stand firm and resist is still necessary, as Anne demonstrated. Establishing our freedom in Christ is not an end. It is a new beginning, and many other character issues will surface as God graciously moves us on from one level of maturity to the next. To stop growing is to stop living.

> Brethren, I do not regard myself as having laid hold of it yet; but one thing I do: forgetting what lies behind and reaching forward to what lies ahead, I press on toward the goal for the prize of the upward call of God in Christ Jesus (Philippians 3:13-14).

3

FREEDOM FROM CULTIC AND OCCULT BONDAGE

W hen I first met Sandy, she was fleeing from a conference session in fear. She is a lovely lady in her early forties, and she has a bubbly personality with enough energy for two. She has a committed Christian husband and five children, and she lives in a beautiful suburban community.

Sandy masked very well the battle that had been raging in her mind for most of her life. Few people, if any, suspected the war going on inside until she mysteriously started withdrawing from church and friends 18 months before we met. Here is her story.

At last I am able to believe I am a child of God. I am now sure of my place in my Father's heart. He loves me. My spirit bears witness with His Spirit that it is so. I no longer feel like I am outside the family of God—I no longer feel like an orphan.

Since I met with Neil during a conference, the evil presence inside me is gone, and the many voices that haunted me for 35 years are also gone. My entire mind feels clean, spacious, and beautiful.

Before I found my freedom in Christ, I lived mostly in a very tiny corner of my mind. Even then I could never escape the commanding voices, filthy language, or accusing anger. So I tried to separate myself from my mind altogether and live a life disassociated from it.

I became a Christian in 1979, but I have struggled continually to

45

believe that God actually accepted me, wanted me, and cared about me. At last this lifelong struggle has come to an end. Before, I could never hear that still, small voice of God in my mind without being punished for it by the other voices. Today, only the still, small voice is there.

It all started when I was very young. My father professed to be an atheist, and my mother was very religious, so our home was filled with conflict and confusion. I went to religious schools, but when I came home I heard from my father that religion was all a lot of nonsense for weak people. I actually hoped that he was correct and that there wasn't any God because I was afraid of my mother's religion. I was afraid that God would get me if I didn't behave correctly. I was looking for spiritual answers even though I rejected both of my parents' beliefs.

Both my home and my mother's parents' home were riddled with superstitious beliefs and good-luck charms. I remember visiting my mother's parents and feeling that their house was a quiet place to get away from the chaos of my own home. Grandma didn't have any toys for me to play with except a Magic 8 Ball. There was a window in the ball and little chips inside with many different answers. I would ask the ball a question, like "Will it rain tomorrow?" One of the answers would float up to the top, such as "Probably."

I grew very attached to that ball and spent a lot of time at my grandmother's house playing with it, believing it had magic power and answers for everything. I communicated with the ball about my parents and what was happening in my life, using it as a fortune-telling device. Many of the answers the ball gave me were correct, reinforcing my belief that the ball had power.

I suppose the grown-ups thought it was just a toy for the grandchildren to play with. When I had problems, though, I stored them up until I got to my grandmother's house and tried to solve them with the Magic 8 Ball. When I visited my father's parents, they took me to their very legalistic church, and I became terrified of hell. Being fearful of God and religion, I turned to the ball to try to predict events. That way I could be prepared in advance for any disasters God was going to send my way.

By the time I was 14, I had become very religious in the Catholic church where, for some reason, I felt safe. At home, my dad's alcoholism and my parents' fighting intensified, and there was no peace. My parents would probably say that I caused the fighting and that I was a problem child. My mother tried to keep my father and me separated because he was very abusive and I was not passive. I loved to fight and always inserted myself between him and anyone he was angry with. He threw me out of the house whenever he saw me, so eventually I came home only when he was away or asleep.

I was so explosively angry and rebellious and hateful of everyone in authority that people were careful to walk around me. What they didn't know was that inside I felt like a sad, lonely, scared little girl. I just wanted someone to take care of me, but I could never share this. When someone attempted to get close to me, I hid my insecurity by becoming argumentative.

I was a problem at school and in the community, and I became sexually promiscuous—basically breaking the Ten Commandments any way I could. Once I went into a Catholic church, looked at the crucifix and said, "Everything You hate, I love; and everything You love, I hate." I was daring God to strike me, and I wasn't even afraid that He might.

At 19 I went to a major city and lived with two other girls for two years. Once, when we were in a bar at two in the morning, a bartender gave us a small calling card and asked, "Why don't you girls go to my church? Maybe you'll find answers to some of your problems and won't have to be out here in the middle of the night." I decided to try the church one more time, believing that all churches were the same. I just wanted to be in a family and feel safe, so the next day we went to that church. I had no idea it was a cult, and for ten years I was involved in it!

Initially, I felt loved; it was my family. They took an interest in my life. No one had paid that much attention to me before. No one had taken enough notice of me to say, "We want you to get nine hours of sleep. We want you to eat three meals a day. We want to know where you are." They held me accountable for my lifestyle, and I interpreted their interest in me as love and concern for my well-being. I would have died for them.

I accepted their philosophy that we are all gods. This fit in with my father's atheistic views that there really is no supreme God and that religion is just somebody's invention to control people. They also explained who Jesus Christ was, and that seemed to satisfy my mother's religion. They said that He was just a good teacher like Muhammad or Buddha but that He wasn't supreme or God. If He were, He could have prevented Himself from having to die on the cross.

The more I got involved, the more the cult consumed my life. I believed everything they said and rejected anything I read in the newspapers or heard on TV. So I read nothing unless the cult wrote it, and I believed nothing unless their signature was on it. My whole world revolved around its teaching.

I went through a lot of personal instruction about becoming a "totally free spiritual being." Because this group taught reincarnation, I believed that I'd had hundreds of past lifetimes. I "learned" previous names, how many children I had, even the color of my hair. This included lives on other planets. Because I trusted them, I believed them. No one else knew this "truth" about themselves simply because they weren't willing to know the truth.

I tried to live in two worlds. From the time I was seven, I heard voices in my head and had invisible friends. I lived in one world at school and another world at home. The voices in my head continued speaking to me. The cult leaders said the voices were from my past lifetimes. My ill-fated hope was that they would be put to rest and not bother me anymore when I was fully instructed.

While this was happening, my family moved to another state, and my mother was invited to a neighborhood Bible study, where she became a born-again Christian. She didn't tell anyone because my father was still an atheist and wouldn't have let her go to the study. But she asked her friends to pray for the conversion of her husband and her kids. Had I known they were praying for me, I would have tried to stop her.

When my mother became ill with cancer, I visited her on her deathbed to convert her. In the next lifetime, she would live in the cult, and I could become aware of her. Then she would have a better life than the one she'd had with Dad.

While visiting her, I felt total hatred for her friends who came to her room, talked about Jesus, and prayed for her healing. I ridiculed their attempts but was astounded by the strength of my mother's convictions. It was a battle between her mind and mine, but one night she was in so much pain and so worn down emotionally that she went through a commitment prayer with me to give her spirit to my cult. Satisfied, I went home the next day, and she died several days later.

I remember playing Scrabble that day with a neighbor at three in the afternoon when suddenly I sensed my mother's presence in the room. I said, "What are you doing here? You should go to headquarters, where you're supposed to be." Later, my brother called and told me that my mother had died around that time.

My friend in the cult told me that everything was fine—they had received my mother's spirit. Eventually, they would call me when the baby was born who would receive my mother's spirit so that I could go to see this baby.

About a week later, I received a letter from one of my mother's friends who had been with her when she died. She said that my mother had gone to be with Jesus. That made me so angry that I went to a local church and stole a Bible. I was going to highlight all of the lies and then send it to this lady to show her how confused she was and to convert her to the cult.

I had never read a Bible before, much less owned one, so I turned to the back to see how it ended. When I read the book of Revelation, I was scared because the cult taught the book of Revelation backward. They said that people were really gods who go back and take their rightful place in heaven.

I went to the church where I stole the Bible and tried to get in touch with my mother's spirit. I figured that if she was a Christian, I should be able to go to a Christian place and contact her. When I got to the church, a middle-aged couple approached me and asked if they could help me in any way. When I told them I was trying to get in touch with my mother, they lovingly said that they didn't think I would find her there, but they invited me to have breakfast with them and talk about it. It turned out to be a Christian fellowship breakfast where, for the first time in my life, I was with a group of people whose lives seemed special because of their relationship with Jesus Christ.

During the next several months, my confusion continued as I went back and forth between my Bible and my cult books. I visited the church where I had met the couple, and they came to my house just to read Scripture with me. I consider them my spiritual mother and father. They never made me feel evil or bad; they just loved and accepted me.

Every month they picked me up and took me to their Christian breakfast and other church services.

During this time, I told God that wherever my mother went was where I wanted to be. If I caused her to lose heaven because of what I did, I didn't want to be a Christian. I wanted to be with her. But if she had really gone to be with Jesus, as her friend who wrote me had said, then I wanted to be there too. I just couldn't choose.

One night I had a dream in which I saw my mother walking toward me with another person in white, and she said, "I forgive you for what you did, and I want you to forgive yourself and to pray for your father." That woke me like a shot. I awakened my husband and said, "I know where she is." I was angry that she had asked me to pray for my father, but that's how I know it was my mother. No one else would dare ask me to do that.

The next week I went to church with that couple, gave my life to the Lord, and renounced my cult involvement. I gave them all of my cult books and paraphernalia, and they took them out of the house. For the next two years I was discipled by them and their fellowship group.

Six weeks after becoming a Christian, I found out that I was pregnant. I was angry with the Lord. I had already had three abortions and decided that I shouldn't have to go through with the pregnancy just because I was a Christian. But my husband said, "I thought you were a Christian and that Christians don't believe in abortions." It angered me that God would speak to me through my husband, who wasn't even a Christian, but God seemed to say to me, *Listen, your home is big enough for a baby. How about your heart? Is it big enough?* I decided to keep the baby.

Nine months after the baby was born, my husband gave his life to the Lord. He said, "When you decided against an abortion, I was impressed by God's intervention and impact in your life."

I wondered if I should become a Catholic, as my mother had been. My spiritual parents said it would be all right to go to the Catholic church, so I went to a charismatic Catholic prayer group. When the priest learned of my background, he suggested that I probably needed deliverance, so I met with him. He started talking to whatever was inside me, asking its name. The "thing" gave him a name and become angry and violent; I became frightened and beat up the priest.

The experience scared me so much that I decided to keep it a secret. I wanted to believe that if I were really a Christian, God would make that horrible presence go away. Because it didn't, I couldn't believe I had a relationship with God. People told me I was saved because I had given my heart to the Lord, but no one could provide the assurance I was looking for. I felt half evil and half good, and I couldn't see how half of me could go to heaven.

We moved again, had more children, and got involved in a new church and new Bible studies. I still lived a divided life. I attended church, but when I came home, the voices tormented me. They were no longer my friends. They were accusing, screaming, angry, and profane. They told me, *You think you're a Christian, but you're not. You're dirty and sinful.* The more I acted like a Christian, the worse the voices became.

I became legalistic, thinking I had to go to every Bible study and church activity. I went Sunday morning, Sunday evening, and Wednesday evening, believing that being present every time the church was open was the only way I could prove I was a Christian.

I went on mission trips and taught Sunday school. When I taught Bible studies and shared the dangers of cults with others, everything inside me became intensified. Anger became rage, the pain became torment, and the accusations made me feel suicidal. I thought, *Why don't I just kill myself? I could never be good enough to be a real Christian.*

When I spoke on a radio program about the dangers of cults, I was plagued with fear that my kids would be killed. I became paranoid about even sending them to school, so I dropped everything. When I withdrew, I temporarily felt better, and the voices lessened, but I became a loner—not going anywhere or talking to anybody, just wanting to be by myself all the time. I felt more and more bound, and my internal life was like a dark prison.

I went to Christian counseling and began sorting out my abusive childhood and putting some things together. I was diagnosed as having a dissociative disorder because of the voices and MPD (multiple personality disorder) because many times I would say, "Well, we feel this way."

"Why are you saying *we?*" my counselor asked.

All I could say was, "I don't know."

This frightened me, but I was also relieved to know that someone believed that voices were inside me. I went to counseling two days a week to relieve the pain and the torment. If we seemed to make progress, I became fearful and punished myself by doing anything dangerous or painful. Nothing quieted the rage inside me except praise and worship songs. Only while listening to them did I feel that I wasn't going crazy. Still, I could only listen, never sing.

The counselors loved me and were faithfully there for me every week. They prayed for me and promised to stay with me for the journey. They felt it would take a long time for me to become integrated. They gave me hope, assuring me that God wanted me to be whole and that He would bring about my healing. I vacillated between hope and despair as if I were on a roller coaster. The Christian counselors were a lifeline for me. I felt God's love and acceptance through their listening, understanding, and caring.

However, we ran up against a wall. When I was seven years old, a traumatic event had occurred, resulting in such tremendous fear that even in counseling I could never progress beyond that point. I would get to the age of seven and then be too afraid to go on. I reasoned, *If it's that bad, I don't want to know what it is.* A voice in my head told me that I would be harmed if I remembered.

My friend and neighbor knew about my struggle. One day she asked me if I would help her prepare for a Resolving Personal and Spiritual Conflicts conference that was coming to her church in about six weeks—visiting churches, putting up posters, and selling the books. I didn't want to do it. I was sure the conference was just one more meeting like the ones I had already tried. Every time I went, I came home lonely and discouraged, knowing I would be punished because I was trying to find a cure. I was afraid my life would become more miserable. Nonetheless, I halfheartedly agreed to help.

My neighbor gave me videos of the conference to preview so I would be able to answer questions about the materials. After watching only ten minutes of the first video, I decided that I hated Neil and that he didn't have anything to say. I felt like telling people not to go and said to my neighbor, "I don't like him. Are you sure you want him to come and give this conference? I think there's something wrong with him."

She replied, "Well, you're the only one who has told me that, and I've talked to about thirty-five people."

At the conference, my resistance increased, and I didn't hear all of what was said. I couldn't remember the nights Neil talked about our identity in Christ, and I sat in the second row, unable to sing any of the hymns. As he spoke, part of me said, *That's not new. We all knew that anyway.* Another little voice inside of me said, *I sure wish that everything he said is true and that he could help me.* But I never revealed that hopeful part, only my critical part. Talking with others I would say, "So what do you think of the conference? It's really not that great, is it?"

Near the end of the week, we saw a video of a two-hour counseling session. I could not watch the woman on the video finding her freedom. I felt fear and anger all at the same time. I started choking, felt sick, and headed for my car to go home, determined not to show up again on Saturday. But Neil was in the hallway between me and my car.

We went into a side room, and Neil walked me through some renunciations in which I verbally repeated a series of statements, taking a stand against Satan and all of his influences in my life. I also prayed that God would reveal to me whatever it was that prevented me from sitting to watch the video—and that's when I remembered what happened when I was seven years old. It was as if the clouds rolled away and I saw myself as a little girl, terrified of a dark, black presence.

I was playing with dolls in the back bedroom of our home. It was daytime, nothing frightening was happening, and no one else was present in the room. But suddenly I felt total fear. I remember stopping my play and lying down, facing the ceiling and saying, "What do you want?" to a huge, black presence that was over me.

The presence said to me, *Can I share your body with you?*

I answered, "If you promise not to kill me, you can."

I actually felt that presence totally infiltrating me from head to toe. It was so oppressive to have this thing go into every pore of my body that I remember thinking I would die. I was only seven, but it was so sexual and so dirty that I felt I had a big secret I had to hide and that I could never tell anyone. From that time on I felt that I had more than one personality, and sharing my body with unseen others seemed natural. Sometimes I would do things and not remember them when people would tell me. And I would think, *Well, that wasn't me. That was my invisible friend who did that.*

I never played with the Magic 8 Ball again. I only spoke with my invisible friend, who suggested things I should do. Sometimes the suggestions were bad, but sometimes they were good. Because I needed companionship in my abusive childhood, I never thought the voice was anything other than a friend.

Neil led me by giving me the words to speak, and I specifically renounced all satanic guardians that had been assigned to me. At that point I was startled by the presence of evil and afraid we would both be beaten up. The presence reminded me that I had played with that Magic 8 Ball for years.

Neil told me not to be afraid and asked what the presence was saying to me. Whenever I told him what the voices were saying, he responded, "That's a lie," and gently led me through the Steps to Freedom in Christ. I can remember the very moment the presence wasn't there anymore. I felt like the small person that was really me was being blown up like a balloon inside me. Finally, after 35 years of fractured living, I was the only person inside. The place that the evil presence vacated is now dedicated to my new occupant: the clean, gentle, quiet Spirit of God.

Saturday morning I was afraid to wake up, thinking, *This isn't real.* I didn't want to open my eyes because usually the voice would say something like, *Get up, you stupid little slut. You've got work to do.* But not that morning. There were no voices at all, and I lay in my bed, thinking, *There's no one here but me.*

When I went back to the conference and walked in the door, people noticed that I looked different. I told them that I had always felt like an orphan in the body of Christ, but now I felt free and part of the family of God.

I thought that as soon as Neil left, this thing was going to come back. But the peace lasted because Jesus Christ is the One who set me free. I practiced the Steps to Freedom in Christ by myself at least four or five more times—whenever I became afraid again. I was convinced that God wanted it gone as much as I did, and it's never been there since.

A week later, my family had a head-on car collision. I was afraid the voice would be there to say, *I'm going to crush you because you think you're free.* Instead I sensed God saying, *I am here to protect you, and I'll always be here like this.*

When one of my girls asked me if the wreck was her fault, I wondered why she felt this way. I remembered that one of the Steps to Freedom in Christ is breaking the ancestral ties because sins of the parents can be passed on from one generation to the next (Exodus 20:4-5). As we talked, my ten-year-old told me, "Sometimes I know things are going to happen before they happen. And sometimes I look out the window and see things that nobody else sees."

Instantly, I knew that my daughter also needed to be released from bondage. So I led her through the Steps, paraphrasing the big words into her language. She renounced all the sins of her ancestors and rejected any way in which Satan might have been claiming ownership of her. She declared herself to be eternally and completely committed to the Lord Jesus Christ. Since then she has never again experienced that demonic presence.

My husband was away during the conference, and when he came home, I told him everything that had happened. The next Sunday, in our Sunday school class, the leader asked if anyone wanted to share about the conference. My husband stood and said, "I want to share even though I wasn't there, because the Lord gave me a new wife to come home to."

Before the conference, I didn't have any positive identity or sense of worth. Every day I felt that God had a measure of mercy for me and that someday it would run out, that even God Himself must wonder why He made me. I just knew that someday He was going to say, *I've had enough of Sandy.* So every day I would pray, *God, please don't let it be today. Let me get this one last thing done before You do it.*

I experienced such freedom when Neil taught that God and Satan are not coequal but that God is off the charts and Satan is way beneath Him. Neil explained that we should not make the mistake of thinking that Satan has divine attributes. I had always thought that God and Satan were coequal, fighting it out for us, and that God was basically saying, *You can have Sandy.* I had cried to God constantly since my conversion,

Create a clean heart in me!
Renew a right spirit in me!
Please don't cast me out of Your presence!
Please don't take Your Holy Spirit from me!

Over and over I had prayed these prayers for myself, agonizing to know the Lord in a warm and personal way but feeling as if I had a relationship with God's back. Now I feel His face toward me and sense His smile.

I don't live in a tiny corner of my mind or outside of my body anymore. I live inside, sharing my mind with only my precious Lord. What a profound difference! There are no words to adequately describe the peace and absence of pain and torment that I now enjoy daily. It's like being blind all those years and now being able to see. Everything is new, precious, and treasured because it doesn't look black. I'm no longer afraid that I'll be punished for every move I make. I'm able to make decisions now and have choices. I am free to make mistakes!

During the past year and a half, whenever anyone touched me, I felt pain or had horrible sexual thoughts. While having sex, I watched from outside my body. When that evil presence claimed to be my husband, I knew why I had always felt like a prostitute, even as a Christian. After exposing that lie and renouncing it (and after 20 years of marriage), I have finally come to understand what it means to be a bride.

I also feel the love from the Bridegroom I will someday see. He has wiped away my tears and answered the cry of my heart. At last I sense a right Spirit inside me, and I know the departed presence was not the presence of God, but of the evil one. I was fearful that God's presence would leave me, but now I know He is with me forever. I now feel clean inside. I continue to go to Christian counseling, and I am making progress. I am learning to face and let go of the past abuse. I am learning to live in community and trust others again after feeling betrayed by my cult experience.

I believe God in His loving-kindness met me at my point of need and ordained the meeting that exposed and expelled the demonic oppression in my life. Now I can continue growing in the family of God. I now am certain I belong to this family, who loves me. God has shown me that He is faithful and able not only to call me from darkness to light but also to keep me and sustain me until the journey ends, when I shall see Him face-to-face. I still face trials, temptations, and the pain of living in a fallen world, but I walk in it sensing the strong heartbeat of a loving Father within. The demonic interference has been removed. Praise the Lord.

We Must Not Be Ignorant of Satan's Schemes

Sandy's life story reveals Satan's hideousness. Would he actually take advantage of a child with dysfunctional parents and grandparents who ignorantly provided occult toys for their grandchildren? Yes, Satan would, and he does.

I have traced the origin of many adult problems to childhood fantasies, imaginary friends, counterfeit guidance, the occult, and abuses. It is not enough to warn our children about the stranger in the street. We need to warn them about the one who may appear in their room. Our research indicates that half of our professing Christian teenagers have had some experience in their room that frightened them.

The Catholic priest's noble but disastrous attempt at an exorcism demonstrates one reason why I don't advocate the power-encounter approach. It can be like sticking a broom handle into a hornets' nest, rattling it around and proclaiming, "Hey, there are demons here!" That kind of experience left Sandy terrorized and reluctant to address the issue again. When the spiritual battle is seen as a truth encounter, you need only work with the person, and you never have to lose control.

The brain is the control center, and as long as Sandy was willing to share with me what was going on inside, we never lost control. Accusing and terrorizing thoughts were bombarding her mind. When she revealed what she was hearing, I simply exposed the deception by saying, "That's a lie" or by asking Sandy to renounce it as a lie and tell it to go away. The power of Satan is in the lie; when the lie is exposed, the power is broken. God's truth sets people free.

Occasionally, I invite a person to ask God to reveal what is keeping him or her in bondage, and often past events and blocked memories come to mind so the person can confess and renounce them. In Sandy's case, she had no conscious memory of what had happened when she was seven.

Her concern about my leaving town is another reason I like to deal only with the person. When she asked me what she was going to do when I wasn't there, I responded, "I didn't do anything. You did the renouncing, and you exercised your authority in Christ by telling the evil presence to go. Jesus Christ is your Deliverer, and He will always be with you." She renounced her invitation to let the demon share her body. Later she renounced all her cult and occult experiences. I cannot overstate how important this step is. It is a critical part of repentance.

From the first century and throughout its history, the church has publicly declared, "I renounce you, Satan, and all your works and all your ways." Catholic, Orthodox, and some liturgical Protestant churches still make that profession. Most evangelical churches don't. That generic statement needs to be applied specifically for each individual. Any dabbling in the occult, involvement with cults, or seeking false guidance must be confessed and renounced. All Satan's works and all Satan's ways need to be renounced as God brings them to our memory. All lies and counterfeit guidance must be replaced by "the way, and the truth, and the life" (John 14:6). This is done in the first of the seven Steps to Freedom in Christ.

Sandy had never had a healthy sexual relationship. She perceived herself as a prostitute because the evil presence claimed to be her husband. Freedom from that bondage allowed her to have a loving, intimate relationship with her husband. I will have much more to say about sexual bondages in later chapters.

The mental battle Sandy suffered is quite typical of those in bondage. Most people caught in a spiritual conflict will talk about their dysfunctional family background or other abuses, but seldom will they reveal the battle going on for their minds. They already fear they are going crazy, and they don't relish the thought of it being confirmed by a pastor or counselor who doesn't understand spiritual warfare. Nor do they like the prospect of taking antipsychotic medication.

Sandy was relieved when her Christian counselor believed her. The secular world has no other alternative than to look for a physical cause and cure because mental illness is the only possible diagnosis. The tragedy of antipsychotic medication (when the problem is actually spiritual) is the drugged state in which it leaves the recipient. How is the truth going to set someone free when the person is so medicated that he or she can hardly talk, much less think?

Many Christian counselors have expressed their appreciation after learning about this spiritual battle and how to resolve it. Such understanding makes their counseling practice much more complete and effective.

In the middle of one conference, a lady shared that I was describing her to a T. She said she was going to a treatment center for 30 days. I asked if I could see her first because I knew that the treatment center she was going to relied primarily on drugs for therapy. She agreed, and later she wrote about her experience.

After meeting with Neil, I was absolutely euphoric, and so was my husband. He was so happy to see me happy. I was finally able to take my position with Christ and renounce the deceiver. The Lord has released me from my bondage.

My big news is that I didn't wake up with nightmares or screams. Instead I woke up with my heart singing! The very first thought that entered my mind was, *Even the stones will cry out,* followed by, *Abba, Father.* The Holy Spirit is alive in me! Praise the Lord! I can't begin to describe how free I feel!

Nightmares and voices may have a spiritual explanation for their origins, and the church bears the responsibility to check out these things. I believe that every pastor and Christian counselor should be equipped to help people with this.

You have nothing to lose by practicing or leading someone else through the Steps to Freedom in Christ. It's just old-fashioned housecleaning that takes into account the reality of the spiritual world. We are simply helping people assume responsibility for their relationship with God. Nobody is accusing anybody of anything, nor do we label anyone. If nothing demonic is going on in someone's life, the worst thing that can happen is that the person will really be ready for Communion the next time it is served!

Sandy's story brings out very well the two most sought-after goals we have with this type of counseling. First, that people will know who they are as children of God—that they are included in God's forever family. Second, that the noise in their heads will be quieted and that they will experience the peace that guards our hearts and our minds, the peace that transcends all understanding (Philippians 4:7).

4

FREEDOM FROM
EATING DISORDERS

I received a call from Jennifer asking if I would spend some time with her if she flew out to California. I agreed to set aside one Monday morning, and after hearing her story, I led her through the Steps to Freedom in Christ. A month later, she wrote to thank me and offer this report.

I have to admit, I felt like nothing happened at the time we prayed and that maybe there wasn't a resolution to my problem. I was wrong. Something really did happen, and I have not had one self-destructive thought or action or compulsion since that day.

I think the process began through my prayers of repentance in the months following my suicide attempt. I don't understand it all, but I know that something is really different in my life and that I feel free today. I haven't cut myself in a month, and that is a true miracle.

I still have a few questions. They have to do with my psychological problems. I was told that I have a chronic manic-depressive, schizo-affective disorder, and I am on lithium and an antipsychotic medication. Do I need these? Am I really chronic?

I always felt during my acting-out periods, which is what my doctors based my diagnosis on, that it was not me but rather some strong power outside myself that drove me to act in self-destructive and crazy ways. The last three times I have quit my lithium, I have become suicidal and ended up in the hospital. I don't want that to happen again! I also had a lot of mood swings even on the pills, but since our visit, I have had none! This makes me wonder if I'm really okay and don't need the pills.

Also, ever since I was a little girl I have never been able to pray; there always seems to be a wall between me and God. I was never very happy and have always felt a sense of fear and uneasiness, like something is wrong.

Jennifer's story is important because it clarifies the need to know who we are as children of God and the nature of the spiritual battle we are in. That one morning we were able to process a lot, and she did achieve a sense of freedom. But does she know who she is as a child of God, and does she know how to maintain her freedom in Christ? Achieving freedom is one issue, but maintaining that freedom is something else.

Within six months Jennifer had returned to many of her old problems. Another year passed before she was desperate enough to call. She decided to fly out again, but this time she attended a whole conference. Here is her story.

In seventh grade my eating disorder started—overeating and then starving. I would babysit and clean out the refrigerator, and then I wouldn't eat anything for three or four days. My focus became my weight; I was obsessed with the need to be thin.

Everything around me seemed like a dream, and everybody appeared to be an actor. I thought, *Someday I will wake up, but I won't know the dreamer.* Nothing seemed real. I lived in a "checked-out" state. I didn't think. When people talked, I looked at them in bewilderment because I wasn't in touch with my mind.

During the day I appeared normal and functioned fairly well in school. Nighttimes were weird with a lot of bad dreams and terror. I wept often because of the voices in my head and the images and nonsense thoughts that often filled my mind. But I never said a word to anyone. I knew people would think I was crazy, and I was terrified that nobody would believe me.

My college years were really hard, filled with routine bingeing and purging. I lost 30 pounds and began fainting and having chest pains. Because I was pathetically thin from anorexia, the skin literally hung on my bones. Finally, I agreed to be hospitalized. I was totally exhausted physically, mentally, and spiritually.

I nearly died. My pulse was 40 when I was admitted, and nurses had trouble finding my blood pressure. My parents were very supportive. The hospital was good, and I had Christian therapists, but they never touched on the spiritual. I was cutting myself, using razor blades and knives. I still have scars on my hands from digging holes into them with my fingernails.

The voices in my head and the nighttimes were bad, with demonic visitations and something raping me at night, holding me down so I couldn't move, or so it seemed. Sometimes I crawled down the hall, trying to get away from what seemed like things flying around my room. I was terrorized; thoughts of cutting my heart out dominated my mind. I did actually cut on my chest with knives because I thought my heart was poison and that I needed to get rid of it so I would be clean.

When childhood memories started to surface, I lost it. I made repeated visits to the hospital and was absolutely out of control. On some days it required five or six people to restrain me. I would be out of my body, watching myself fighting and kicking until they would sedate me. I was diagnosed as manic-depressive. I took lithium and continued with antidepressants for the next six years, and those did quiet me somewhat.

While I was in the hospital, a friend suggested that I talk with Neil, but I told her no. The thought of demonic influence was terrifying to me, and I told her, "God said if two or more people pray He would listen. Why can't several people just pray with me here in the hospital? Why do I need somebody else to come?"

I talked with my Christian counselors, and they said, "Your friends just want to make this a spiritual matter because they don't want to deal with the pain in your life." The counselors had gained my trust that year, so I believed them and refused to see Neil. That's the first time I ever heard Neil's name. I did not meet him for three years. I was too afraid; the whole idea freaked me out.

Somehow I graduated and started working. I would do a fantastic job at work and then get in my car, pull out my razor blades, and live in a different world for the next 16 hours. Then I would go back to work. I was talking with all of my "friends" in my head and ritualistically cutting myself for the blood. I just wanted to feel; I knew I was not in touch with reality.

At night I would often lie awake, hoping I would die before morning. I wrote suicide notes and knew every empty house around. These were houses that were for sale, where I could drive my car into the garage, leave the motor running, and kill myself. I also knew the gun shops in town and their hours so I could get a gun if I needed one. I kept 200 or 300 pills at home so I always had an "out" for when I could bear it no longer. I had many plans to commit suicide.

I kept thinking, *The Lord has got to get me through this.* I knew He was my only hope and that there was a reason to live, so I kept crying out to Him. I remember crawling into a corner of my room at night and sleeping there on the floor. I was trying to get away from it all and praying to God that I could get through one more night. I prayed that He would give me strength and protect me from myself. I blamed myself for all of this.

I feared for my life, and so did many of my friends. I went to see a pastor and told him that I thought I had a spiritual problem and that I felt like I was going to die. He said, "You have one of the best psychiatrists in town; I don't know why you're talking to me." Then he asked, "Are you taking your medicine?" He was afraid of me and he didn't know how to help me.

Once I spent several hours talking with some caring friends. One suggested, "Jennifer, you just need to go into the throne room of Jesus." The voices inside me said, "That's it!" To me, "going into the throne room" meant to die. I drove to a hotel, went to a room, and took 200 pills. I lay down by my simple note that read, "I'm going home to be with Jesus. I just can't take it anymore."

I called someone because I didn't want to be alone when I died. I felt that if there was someone on the other end of the phone it would help. At first I wouldn't give the phone number to my friend, but later I was so sleepy and out of it that I gave in so I could go to sleep and my friend could call me back later. Two and a half hours later they found me and took me to a hospital, where my stomach was pumped and I was admitted to the intensive care unit. I should have died, but by a miracle of God, I didn't.

I was hospitalized again in a different Christian clinic. The possibility of my problem being spiritual was never addressed. I was diagnosed as being schizo-affective and bipolar-depressive. The doctors told me that

I didn't know reality and that I needed to base my confidence on what others said and not on what was going on in my head. They told me I would be dependent on medication for the rest of my life. The side effects of the antipsychotics and antidepressants were horrendous. The tremors were so bad that I had trouble even using my hand to write my name, and my vision was blurred. I was so drugged I couldn't even hold my mouth open.

In counseling I told them I was hearing voices, but they never explored the possibility of them being demonic. They did tell me that since I'd had a lot of therapy already, they wanted to deal with me on the spiritual level. They brought in a godly man who was good, but I couldn't hear or remember a word he said. As soon as he opened his Bible and started to talk, I began listening to other things and planning to kill myself. I felt that if I could just get out of there I would do it, and this time I would be successful.

One day a friend called me at the clinic and honestly addressed the sin in my life. He basically told me I was being manipulative, dishonest, hateful, attention-seeking, and selfish. That was heavy stuff, but he spoke kindly and I was at a point where I was ready to hear it. I got on my knees and wrote a letter to God in my journal asking forgiveness. Those sins were a part of me that I was ashamed of, and I had lived with the guilt of them all my life. I did experience some release, and I know that was the beginning of my healing.

Friends invited me to California for a visit, and I decided I wanted to meet Neil. I went to his office, where we talked for about two hours. He opened his Bible and was going through the Scriptures, but the voices were so loud I couldn't hear a word he said. It was like he was talking gibberish—his words were like another language. That's how it always was with me when people were using the Bible.

I got through the Steps to Freedom in Christ, but I didn't feel any different when I left. I wondered if the words just went straight from my eyes to my mouth without me internalizing anything I was reading. But two areas improved. The struggle with food was better, and I never cut myself again. The voices were also gone for a couple of weeks, but then they came back. I didn't remember Neil saying what to do when the voices and thoughts came back, and it never occurred to me that I didn't have to listen. I didn't know I had a choice, so I got hit worse than ever.

Six months later I was in the hospital again, both suicidal and psychotic. I was out of it and did everything the voices were telling me to do. I was encouraged to see Neil again, but if that didn't work I knew I was going to die. All of this had been going on for seven terrible years, and the side effects of the drugs were so bad that all I did was work four hours and then sit in front of the TV or sleep. I couldn't carry on a meaningful conversation with anybody, and I really didn't care about anything anymore. I felt hopeless, exhausted, and discouraged.

I went to the conference on Resolving Personal and Spiritual Conflicts. I again met with Neil, and at one point I got so sick that I threw up. He introduced me to a lady with a past similar to mine. She sat beside me and prayed for me, so I was more able to hear and comprehend what Neil was saying.

I learned a lot about the spiritual battle that was going on for my mind and what I needed to do to take a stand. Once that part became clear, I was free. I knew what to do and how to do it. Previously, I didn't know how to stay free and walk in my freedom even though I was raised in a good Christian home. I had accepted Christ when I was four, but I never knew who I was in Christ, and I didn't understand the authority I had as a child of God.

I told my psychiatrist that I was free in Christ now and wanted to get off my medication. He said, "You've tried this before, and look at your history."

"But it's different now," I said. "Will you support me in this?" When he said no, I replied, "Well, I'm going to do it anyway. I'll take responsibility for myself."

He said he would see me in a month. I came back in a month and was functioning on half of the prescription, and in two months I was off completely. He asked how I felt, and when I told him I was fine, he shook my hand and said I wouldn't need to come back anymore. It was like I was discovering life for the first time, and I felt impressed to write the following letter to Neil:

Dear Neil,

I was reading back over my journals from years past and was harshly reminded of the darkness and evil in which I was engulfed for so many years. I often wrote about "them" and the control "they" had of me. I often felt that I would rather rest in the darkness than be torn between Satan and God. I didn't realize that I was a child of God and alive in Christ. I thought I was hanging between two spirits, so often I felt that I was being controlled and was crazy, having lost all sense of self and reality. I think in a way I had learned to like the darkness. I felt safe there and was deceived by the lie that if I let go of the evil, I would die and God would not meet my needs or care for me the way I wanted.

This is why I would not talk with you the first time. I didn't want you to take away the only thing I had. I felt sheer terror at the thought. I guess the evil one had something to do with those thoughts and fears. I was so deceived. I really tried to pray and read the Bible, but it all made little sense. Once I tried to read *The Adversary* by Mark Bubeck, and I literally could not make my hand pick it up. I just stared at it.

Psychiatrists tried many different medications and doses (including large doses of antipsychotics) to make things better. I took up to 15 pills a day just to remain in control and somewhat functional. I was so drugged, I couldn't think or feel much at all. I felt like a walking dead person! The therapists and doctors all agreed I had a chronic mental illness that I would deal with for the rest of my life—a very defeating prognosis to hear!

Just weeks before your conference, I had decided that I did not want to entertain the darkness any longer and that I really wanted to get well, but I had no idea how to take that step. Well, I learned how at the conference. I saw the total picture, and once again my head became quiet. The voices stopped, the doubts and confusion lifted, and I was free. Now I know how to stand.

I feel like a small child who has been through a horrible and terrifying storm, lost in confusion and loneliness. I knew my loving Father was on the other side of the door and that He was my only hope and relief, but I could not get through that strong door. Then someone told me how to turn the knob and told me that because I was God's child, I had all the authority and right to open the door. I have reached up and opened the door and run to my Father, and now I am resting in His safe and loving arms. I know

and believe that "neither death, nor life, nor angels, nor principali-
ties, nor things present, nor things to come, nor powers, nor height,
nor depth, nor any other created thing, will be able to separate us
from the love of God" (Romans 8:38-39).

I am working in ministry now, taking tons of time to read and pray
and be loved by the God I had heard so much about but never
experienced. I am giving and sharing and serving in ways I have
always dreamed of doing. In bondage, I could never reach beyond
my desperate self. Now I feel peaceful and full inside, somewhat
childlike, with purpose and direction, joy and hope.

Now when I get accusing or negative thoughts, they just bounce
off because I have learned to bind Satan with one quick sentence,
ignore his lies, and choose the truth. It works! Because of my
strong Savior, Satan leaves me alone almost instantly. I've had a few
pretty down days, but when I do, I choose to remember who I am
and tell Satan and his demons to leave. It's a miracle; the cloud lifts!

My sadness has come when I realize I have lived most of my life
in captivity, believing lies. I try to remember, "For this purpose I
have raised you up, that I may show My power in you, and that My
name may be declared in all the earth" (Exodus 9:16 NKJV). I know
God will use my experiences mightily in my own life as well as in
others'. The chains have fallen off. I have chosen the light and life.

Because of the obvious changes in my countenance, people have
been seeking me out for light and truth. I can't keep up with who
has which of your CDs. I have shared them a lot with others who
find themselves in bondage and need.

I am still seeing a Christian counselor, and this has been very helpful. It's horrendous coming out of my past, and it's a struggle learning how to live. My biggest temptation is to be sick because I got
a lot of strokes from that. I needed to see that I am not a sick person, but a child of God, and that He desires for me to be free. It
was difficult for me to accept that new identity. A few times I have
had "crazy" days. But I realize that this is not what I want, so I call
my friend to pray with me and help me renounce the darkness.

My biggest fight is to stay single-minded because my tendency is
to let my mind split off. My prayer every day is that God will help

me to stay focused and that I will love Him with all my heart and soul, not just a part of it.

Another important friend is a woman who was set free five years ago from being a New Age medium. She has been a tremendous help, but my main support is the friend I met at your conference. Our phone bills are huge, and we see each other three or four times a year. I really don't think I would have made it and stayed free those first couple of months without her.

My family and the treatment I received were the best. They did everything they knew to love me, help me, and save my life. I have been so loved throughout my life by so many friends and family members. I feel it is because of their prayers, consistent love, and support that I am alive today.

I firmly believe that the prescription drugs were what kept me from being able to think or fight. They left me in such a passive, semi-alert state that I couldn't concentrate. I couldn't write because of horrible hand tremors, I couldn't see at times because of blurred vision, and I couldn't concentrate enough to pray. I never had the energy to discern thoughts or remember truths in Scripture, and I couldn't follow conversations. I felt as if I were on 12 or 15 antihistamine tablets at one time—a very helpless condition with no quality of life.

I have written out a ton of truth verses on cards that I carry everywhere. There have been times when the dark cloud of oppression is so crushing. That's when I pull out my cards and read them aloud until the light dispels the darkness and I'm able to pray again. Then I can find the lie I've been believing, claim the truth, announce my position in Christ, and renounce the devil. The process has become so routine that I find myself claiming truth and renouncing lies under my breath, almost without thinking.

My friend and I have talked often of an active surrender. How do I acknowledge my total dependence upon God and fight at the same time? I don't totally understand it, but this active surrender sets us free.

My most difficult struggle to this day is to want to be free. I'm tempted to use my dissociative "alters" for friends. They occupied the places in my split-off self where I used to go to escape reality and find relief. Satan takes advantage of those mental escapes, playing havoc in my mind and life.

I actually buried stones in the ground representing each split-off piece of my mind that I had held on to. In one sense, it was a huge loss. In another, I knew I had to do that because those identities and psychotic-like splits were homes where Satan and his workers resided. I still am tempted, and even have returned to those states when I am under stress, but I keep fighting and am able to bounce back. I'm grasping for God's love and strength in a way I never have been able to before. I now desire to find my safety in Him.

I cannot express the difference in my heart and life. Where my heart used to reside in pieces, now it is whole. Where my mind was void, now there is a song and an intellect beyond anything I could have previously comprehended. Where there was a life of unreality and despair, now there is joy and freedom and light. To God be the glory because all I have done is to finally say yes to His offer of freedom. I am grateful to be alive!

                                                                    Jennifer

Getting and Staying Free

When Jennifer saw me the first time, I led her through the Steps to Freedom in Christ. The fact that there was some resolution was clear from the first letter she sent. However, one three-hour counseling session does not afford enough time for me or anyone else to educate sufficiently regarding our identity in Christ, much less the nature of the spiritual battle. I also didn't have the experience base then that I do now. Since Jennifer lacked this knowledge, she slipped back into her old habit patterns. In her second visit, she participated in an entire conference that provided the information she needed to experience her freedom in Christ and maintain it.

Most pastors can't afford the time to sit one-on-one with people for extended teaching sessions. I usually ask people to read *Victory over the Darkness* and *The Bondage Breaker* before we meet for our first session. If they struggle with reading, as Jennifer did (which is often a symptom of demonic harassment), I take them through the Steps to Freedom in Christ first and follow up with assignments, such as reading portions of the books or listening to recorded messages on the same subjects. Some prefer to listen to the recordings instead of reading the books. It is important that they have a faith base for their walk with Christ.

I don't assume anything regarding spiritual conflicts. People need a safe place to check out spiritual possibilities, just as they need medical professionals to check their bodies. The church must accept the responsibility to offer sound spiritual diagnosis and effective resolution.

Effective counseling is not something you do for another person. You may even be successful in casting out a demon, but it could very possibly return, and the final state could be even worse. When Jennifer did her own confessing, renouncing, forgiving, and so on, she learned the nature of the battle by going through the process. Instead of bypassing her mind, where the real battle was, I appealed to her mind and helped her to assume responsibility for choosing truth.

Jennifer's comments on prescription drugs are appropriate. Using drugs to cure the body is commendable, but using drugs to cure the soul is deplorable. Her ability to think was so impaired that she couldn't process anything. I am often extremely frustrated from seeing people in this condition. However, I never go against the advice of a medical doctor. I strongly caution people not to go off prescription drugs too fast, or serious side effects are likely to occur. Jennifer did go off too quickly after her first visit with me, and that may have contributed to her subsequent relapse. Brain chemistry adjusts to medication, and stopping the medication cold turkey will precipitate symptoms of withdrawal, which patients will probably interpret as the original problem coming back. These patients are therefore likely to return immediately to the medication.

Some People Don't Want Freedom

Spiritually healthy people often have a hard time understanding that others may not always want to get free from their lifestyle of bondage. I have come across many people who don't want to get rid of their "friends." After walking through the Steps to Freedom in Christ with a pastor's wife, I sensed that her freedom wasn't complete. She looked at me and asked, "Now what?"

I paused for a moment and said, "Tell it to go."

A quizzical look came to her face, and she responded, "In the name of the Lord Jesus Christ, I command you to leave my presence." Instantly she was free. The next day she confided that the presence was saying to her mind, *You're not going to just send me away after all the years we have been together, are you?* It was playing on her sympathy.

A young man said a voice was pleading not to make him go because it didn't want to go to hell. The demon wanted to stay so it could go to heaven with him. What a lie! I asked the young man to pray, asking God to reveal the true nature of the voice. As soon as he had finished praying, he cried out in disgust. I really don't know what he saw or heard, but the evil nature of it was very obvious. These are not harmless spirit guides; they are counterfeit spirits seeking to discredit God and promote allegiance to Satan. They are destroyers who will tear apart an individual life, a family, a church, or a ministry.

Bingeing and Purging

Eating disorders are a modern-day plight. The sick philosophies of our society have given godlike status to the body. Young girls are often obsessed with appearance as the standard of their worth. Instead of finding their identity in Christ, they find it in their appearance. Rather than focus on the development of character, they focus on appearance, performance, and status. Satan capitalizes on this misguided pursuit of temporal happiness and self-esteem.

Compounding the problem is the rise of sexual abuse and rape. Many girls and young women who are addicted to eating disorders have been sexually victimized. Lacking a gospel, the secular agencies have no way to completely free these people from their past. Knowing who they are in Christ and the necessity of forgiveness is what brings freedom, but they still have to deal with the lies Satan has been using on them.

One young lady was taking 75 laxatives a day. Being a graduate of an excellent Christian college, she wasn't stupid. Yet reasoning with her had proved futile. Eating disorder clinics had stemmed the tide of weight loss by using strong behavioral controls, but that will not resolve the internal conflicts. When I talked with her I asked, "This has nothing to do with eating, does it?"

"No," she responded.

"You're defecating to purge yourself from evil, aren't you?"

She nodded in agreement.

I asked her to repeat after me: "I renounce defecating in order to purge myself of evil, and I announce that only the blood of Jesus cleanses me from all unrighteousness." As soon as she prayed that prayer, she began to sob. After she regained her composure several minutes later, I asked her what she was thinking. "I can't believe the lies I was believing," she replied. Another woman said she had purged all her life, just as her mother had. She said that she did not consciously plan to do it and that she and her teen daughters had a little joke that she could vomit into a paper cup while driving and never cross the centerline. When I asked her why she was throwing up, she said she felt cleansed afterward. I asked her to repeat after me, "I renounce the lie that throwing up will cleanse me. I believe only in the cleansing work of Christ on the cross."

She repeated that confession and immediately cried out, "Oh my God, that's it, isn't it? Only Jesus can cleanse me from my sin." She said that she saw in her mind a vision of the cross.

This is why people cut themselves, excessively defecate, and purge. They are trying to cleanse themselves of evil. It's a spiritual counterfeit, a lie of Satan, that we can be the gods of our lives and effect our own cleansing. It also illustrates what Paul teaches in Romans 7:15-25. Paul says that evil is present in me even though I want to do good. Cutting, purging, and defecating will not get rid of the evil.

Remember the 450 prophets of Baal who came up against Elijah? They cut themselves (1 Kings 18:28). If you travel around the world, you will still witness many worshippers cutting themselves during pagan religious ceremonies. Revealing that lie and renouncing it is critical. In many cases, people don't even know why they do it, so asking them to explain may be counterproductive. Jennifer was trying to cut out her heart, believing that it was evil. She also shared that she was cutting herself to get in touch with reality, believing that live people bleed.

It is important to note that not all of those who cut themselves have eating disorders, and many who have eating disorders don't cut themselves.

I received an insightful letter from a lady who found tremendous release by going through the Steps to Freedom in Christ, but the pastor had not addressed her eating disorder at that time. Here is part of it.

Dear Neil,

I just finished reading *The Seduction of Our Children*, which I found very eye-opening in many areas. In chapter 13, I was reading through the Steps to Freedom in Christ for children when I noticed a separate section for eating disorders. As I was reading, my heart was pierced with a severe pain, yet there was also a sigh of relief. Your words described what my life has been like since grade school.

Earlier this year I went through the Steps with a pastor, and I was a totally different person. Yet the one thing that didn't seem right was the struggle I was continuing to have with my physical appearance. That subject hadn't come up during my counseling session.

As I read your description of a typical person with an eating disorder, I just wept before the Lord. I started by cutting myself, and then I became anorexic and then bulimic. Eventually I combined all three destructive behaviors.

I read your material about renouncing and announcing, and I agreed with a friend in prayer about it.* God is so good to me. For whatever reason, it was overlooked in earlier counseling. The enemy meant it for evil and kept me in bondage for most of my life. God used your book to add this step of freedom in my life. Thank you so much.

The Need to Be Believed

People who struggle with disorders like these are desperately looking for others who will believe them, people who understand what is going on. They know enough not to share too much about the bizarre thoughts and images with people who don't understand. In Jennifer's case, when she finally did share part of her story, people didn't really believe her, and some don't to this day. They see her wholeness as a fluke. Pastors and counselors must recognize the reality of the spiritual world and come to terms with the truth that "our struggle is not against flesh and blood, but against the rulers, against the powers, against the world forces of this darkness, against the spiritual forces of wickedness in the heavenly places" (Ephesians 6:12).

Aftercare

Jennifer's thoughts on aftercare are on target. The need to have a friend to call and be accountable to can't be stressed enough. God never intended for

---

*   That prayer is in the present edition of *The Steps to Freedom in Christ.*

us to live alone; we need each other. And Jennifer needed to continue with counseling to help her adjust to a new way of living. In many ways, she had not developed as others do, and she needed to mature into wholeness. Freedom does not constitute maturity. People like Jennifer are developing new habits in their thinking, and reprogramming their minds takes some time.

Her counselors are good people who would have done anything to help her, and they provided her with the support she needed to survive. Nobody has all the answers. First and foremost, we need the Lord, but we also need one another.

Effective Prayer for Others

Think of the pastors who try to help people like Jennifer. Most haven't had formal training in counseling, and few have been trained to deal with the kingdom of darkness. Even those who have taken extended courses in counseling would be unlikely to be able to help someone like Jennifer because of the secular influence that dominates the field of psychology. Desperate people come with overwhelming needs, knowing that their only hope is the Lord. Sometimes the only pastoral weapon at their disposal is prayer, so they pray. But often they see very little happen in response, which can be very discouraging. Let's consider some reasons why this might be.

The sufferer is responsible to pray. Most Christians are aware of the passage in James that instructs those who are sick to call the elders, who are to pray and anoint with oil. I believe the church should be doing this, but we often overlook much of what James says. He begins with this: "Is anyone among you suffering? Then he must pray" (5:13). Initially, the person who needs to pray is the sufferer. When I was a pastor, hurting people often asked me to pray for them. Of course, I was happy to, but I saw very few answers to prayer. When it comes to resolving personal and spiritual conflicts, the only effective prayer is the prayer of a repentant heart.

After leading a social worker through the Steps to Freedom in Christ, the change in her countenance was so noticeable that I encouraged her to visit the restroom and take a good look in the mirror. She was glowing when she returned to my office. As she reflected on the resolution of her spiritual conflicts, she said, "I always thought somebody else had to pray for me." That is a very common misconception. In the Steps, the inquirer is the one doing most of the praying.

We can't have a secondhand relationship with God. We may need a third party to facilitate the reconciliation of two personalities, but they won't be reconciled by what the facilitator does. They will only be reconciled by the concessions made by the principal parties. In spiritual resolution, God doesn't make concessions in order for us to be reconciled to Him. The Steps to Freedom in Christ lay out the "concessions" we have to make in order to assume our responsibility.

The sufferer is responsible to seek healing. "Is anyone among you sick? Then he must call for the elders of the church" (5:14). Notice that the one who is sick is responsible to take the initiative. We will never see victory in our churches unless our people accept the responsibility for their own physical and spiritual well-being. We can't heal hurting people who don't want to get well. The Steps to Freedom in Christ work only if the inquirers want to be well and will assume their own responsibility.

Mark records the incident when Jesus sent His disciples on ahead of Him in a boat. The wind came up, and the disciples ended up in the middle of the sea, "straining at the oars." As Jesus walked on the sea, "He intended to pass by them" (Mark 6:48). In much the same way, Jesus intends to pass by the self-sufficient. If we want to row our own boat, He will let us strain at the oars until our arms fall off. When the disciples cried out, He came to them. When the sick call the elders, they should also come.

The sufferer is responsible to confess. James continues, "Therefore, confess your sins to one another, and pray for one another so that you may be healed. The effective prayer of a righteous man can accomplish much" (5:16). Our prayers for others will be most effective after they have confessed their sins. The Steps to Freedom in Christ are a fierce moral inventory. I have heard people confess incredible atrocities as they go through the Steps. My role is to assure them that God answers prayer and forgives His repentant children.

I am most confident in prayer after I have taken a person through the Steps. When seeking resolution, the proper order is to seek first God's kingdom and His righteousness, and then all the other things will be added to us (Matthew 6:33). John writes, "The one who practices sin is of the devil; for the devil has sinned from the beginning. The Son of God appeared for this purpose, to destroy the works of the devil" (1 John 3:8). I believe we are perfectly in God's will when we ask Him to restore a life damaged by the influences of Satan. That damage could be physical, emotional, or spiritual.

A young lady approached me in a conference with a cheerful "Hi!"

"Hi yourself," I responded.

"You don't recognize me, do you?" she asked. I didn't, and even after she reminded me that I had counseled with her a year earlier, I still didn't recognize her—she had changed that much! Like Jennifer, her appearance and countenance were totally different, a beautiful demonstration of change in a person who seeks God's kingdom first. What a difference freedom in Christ makes!

5

Female Sexual Abuse and Freedom

Many defeated Christians are caught in a cycle that goes like this: sin, confess, sin, confess, sin, confess, sin...give up. It is most common in sexual bondages. This cycle of defeat is destined to continue downward for two reasons. First, confession is the initial step toward repentance, but it is not complete repentance. Second, God and the individual are not the only two players in this eternal struggle between good and evil. Satan and his evil workers are very active players. In fact, "the whole world lies in the power of the evil one" (1 John 5:19).

Suppose you are standing in front of a closed door. On the other side, a talking dog is saying, "Come on, let me in. You know you want to. Everybody does it. Nobody will know. You will get away with it." On the other side of the door, he is the tempter. If you yield to that temptation, you have opened the door. The dog's jaw is now clamped around the calf of your leg, and he changes his role to that of an accuser: "You opened the door. You opened the door." If you could see the true picture, would you beat on yourself or the dog? If we don't understand the spiritual battle, we will buy his accusations and condemn ourselves, and a few well-meaning Christians may also add their accusations.

Painfully aware that we left the door open to sin, we cry out to God for forgiveness. Guess what God does—He forgives us! Actually, we are already forgiven. Confessing isn't asking for forgiveness; rather, confessing is acknowledging, "I did it." It is critically important that we confess to God and admit that we opened the door (we sinned). But that is not enough because the dog is still there and the door is still open. Rather than continuing the cycle of sin and confession, sin and confession, we should use a more complete process: confess, repent, resist, and stand firm. In other words, "Submit therefore to God. Resist the devil and he will flee from you" (James 4:7).

If you and God are the only two players, one of you will have to take the rap for an awful lot of havoc in this world. God is certainly not the author of confusion and death. In fact, He is the author of life. The god of this world is the chief architect of rebellion, sin, sickness, and death. He is the father of lies (John 8:44).

However, our theological thinking or practice should never lead us to say, "The devil made me do it." There will be no victory for those who will not admit that they opened the door and assume responsibility for their own attitudes and actions. We are responsible to not let sin reign in our mortal bodies (Romans 6:12). Nonetheless, treating those in bondage as the principal culprits and throwing them out because they can't get their act together is the height of pharisaic judgment and human rejection. Tragically, those most inclined to judge others are usually those most incapable of helping.

If you witnessed a little girl being sexually molested because she left the door open and evil intruders took advantage of her carelessness, would you overlook the abusers and confront only the girl? If you did, the little girl would conclude that there was something evil about herself and that she had nowhere to turn for help. That's what Nancy and many others like her have experienced. Let's learn from her story.

> Both my parents were young and non-Christians. They had been married two years when I was born, and their marriage was rocky. Later, two brothers and a sister were added, and photos from that time made us look like a normal, happy family. My dad was handsome, and my mother was attractive. Mostly the pictures are of the family all dressed up for church on Easter Sunday. We never went any other time.
>
> We moved a lot, and I attended eight different schools before attending two different high schools. My father had a drug and alcohol problem and was in and out of jail for stealing to buy the things he needed in order to feed his addiction. He even broke open my piggy

bank for whatever money I had, and once he sold all the lamps in the house. He sometimes left for a couple of days at a time and then came home smashed and abusive, breaking furniture, pictures, and glassware. This was not uncommon; whenever my father got mad, things were destroyed.

My father told me when I was three years old that I could sleep in his room while my mother was at work. I remember lying in my parents' bed and my dad talking to me like I was his wife. He would tell me that he loved me more than he did my mother and that I was his special girl. Then he would touch me sexually. I really had no idea what was going on, only that this made Daddy happy and then he would be nice to me. He told me that I should never tell my mother about this because she wouldn't understand. It was then that I started masturbating, usually several times a day.

This was a confusing time for me. Sometimes I was torn between my parents, but on other nights, when my mother was home, my father would beat me and throw me against the wall. One night he took a blanket and threw it over my entire body and then sat on the blanket. I couldn't breathe or see any light. At first my mother just laughed, but then she yelled at my dad and told him to get up. That experience was one of the first times I remember being outside of myself and watching what was going on.

Another time, my dad got my baby brother and me drunk. He gave us tastes of whatever he was drinking and then spun us around and watched us try to walk.

About every two or three months my mom would leave my dad, and we would spend some time at my grandparents' home until my dad would say, "I'm sorry; I won't ever do it again." So we would move back in with him. During those times of separation I would always be with my mom, and I was glad. I was so afraid of being totally alone with my father.

One time when I was about five, Dad came home and started breaking furniture and pictures, but this time was different. It was late at night, and Mom and I were up, but we were not packing to leave as we often did. On this particular night, we were crouched in a corner of their bedroom. The house was totaled, worse than usual, and my dad was standing over us with a gun pointed at my mother's head. He said, "This is it, I'm going to pull the trigger." My mom hugged me tightly and pleaded with him not to kill her. I was crying, and I heard the trigger snap, but no explosion. Mom had thrown away the bullets, and the gun that my dad thought was loaded was empty, although Mom wasn't sure whether he had gotten more bullets or not.

My dad became even more angry and picked up my mom and threw her across the room. Mom told me to run next door, so I did. The police came and took my dad away, and I stayed at the neighbors' house, sleeping in a strange bed all alone and crying like I had never cried before. I wanted my mom to hold me, but she wasn't there. I don't know where she went, but whenever things got really bad I always had to stay somewhere else without my mom. I still don't understand where she went and why she didn't want me with her.

Another time, my dad had a knife, my mother had a broken bottle, and they were fighting. I remember battling in my mind about which one I wanted to win. I loved my mom, but I never felt that she loved me. I knew my dad loved me, but he scared me. That time, Dad cut Mom's throat and beat her up, and a neighbor had to take her to the hospital, where she stayed for several days. I was at a friend's house—alone again.

I thought my parents loved animals more than people. One time my dad brought home a dog that had been mistreated. My parents felt so bad for this dog—they loved him, fed him extra food, and talked about how awful his past owners had been. I remember being jealous of the dog, wishing that my parents would treat me as well as they treated the dog.

By the time I was six, my dad had been in and out of jail several times, and my mother finally left him. We moved in with my grandparents for a couple of years and then into another house in the same town.

I talked to myself constantly, saying how much I needed to masturbate in order to feel better. I would dream of boys in class at school and pretend we were making love. One time I was masturbating while watching television, and my mother came into the room and watched. I didn't see her at first, but when I did, she just smiled at me and told me this was normal.

There were times in the bathtub when I would travel outside of myself and dream I was drowning myself. It felt both good and scary all at the same time. I'd fill up the tub as high as I could, get in and see myself under the water face-up, dead.

I spent as much time as I could at my grandmother's house and saw strange things: shadows coming out of Grandma's closet, voices and noises, and things moving around the room. Once I thought I saw my toy broom fly across my bedroom. These things startled me at first, but after a while I enjoyed trying to make things move myself.

My grandmother gave me a Ouija board, and my brother and I played with it. It was about this time that I asked my brother to sleep with me, and we kissed and held hands. I loved him so much and felt there was no other way to really show him that I cared. (Oh, how I hate you, Satan!)

I was given a dog and would look at him and think, *I love you truly.* I would let him lick me, and for a while it would feel good, but then I would get depressed. One day, I looked at him and wondered what it would be like for him to be dead. Only a few minutes later, he ran out in the road and was hit by a car and killed instantly. I remember having dreams come true as well.

When I was about seven, I attended a neighborhood church. I enjoyed the songs and the people seemed so nice, but I can't remember anyone ever asking who I was or why I was there by myself.

My grandmother and grandfather didn't sleep together. I learned later that my grandfather had an affair and that my grandmother had said he could stay, but they never slept together again. So I would sleep with my grandmother. She wrote stories and would tell them to me, usually stories about friendly ghosts. So I thought the ghosts I was seeing in her house were good.

My grandfather loved me and told me I was his favorite grandchild. I slept with him too, but he never touched me inappropriately or yelled at me or hurt me in any way. We would talk together at the dinner table and play games together, and he would play his guitar and sing for me. Even though there were strange things at their house, this was the closest thing to a happy family in my experience.

My mother remarried, and we moved away. The first few years of their marriage seemed normal. We got spankings, but not beatings. I was in Brownies, I took tap dancing and gymnastics classes, and I did well at school. I still heard voices saying, *You're ugly and stupid. This is going to end, and your real father is going to come and get you.*

I started having dreams about dying and would lie in bed crying out to God for help. *Please let there be something other than death, something beyond death.* I dreamed that my grandparents were going to die, that I would never see them again. I dreamed my mother would die. It became such an obsession that I couldn't get to sleep unless I thought of someone in my family dying, and then I would cry myself to sleep.

I went to a church with a Christian friend and went forward during the altar call, wanting so much for someone to love me and help me, but this was not the time or the place. The counselor said that I needed to be "slain under the cross" so that I could speak in another language. My friend said that I would fall over afterward and that I shouldn't be afraid.

There were about 30 people around me who all started to pray, some in tongues and some not. It was hot and I just wanted to go home, so I thought I would talk some gibberish and fall over, which I did. Everyone was so excited that I was now a "Christian." I knew I had fooled them and was confused, wondering if Christians were fakes.

While in grade school, I had a babysitter only a few years older than me who would take off her clothes and my clothes, and we would lie on each other on the living room floor. Sometimes I spent the night at her house and she would play with me, naked.

In the summers I visited my grandparents' home. The summer after I finished fifth grade, I took a friend with me. I had never had homosexual desires before, but that summer it was different. We played in the greenhouse, and I told her she was my wife, or I hers, and we would hold hands and kiss. One thing led to another, and we would end up on the floor rolling around together until I would end up masturbating. I don't think she ever did, and she seemed scared, but she was always willing to play the game several times a day.

When we returned home, we went into the bushes and tried the game again, but this time it didn't seem right, and we never did it again. We stayed friends throughout our school years but never again mentioned our summer together.

The next year I took another friend to Grandmother's house. This time we stayed in the bedroom and read magazines and acted out the stories in them.

By the time I was in junior high, my mom and stepfather were fighting more and more. I felt guilty about their fights but even worse about my masturbation problem. I couldn't tell anyone or ask if this was normal, though I already knew it couldn't be. I tried my hardest to stop, but there was always that voice saying, *No, it's all right. Everyone does it.* Then, afterward, the same voice would say, *You fool. You are so stupid and ugly, no one will want you.*

When I was in high school, lying became a big part of my life. I wanted to have friends and fun, but I saw myself as stupid and inferior, so I would make up stories to make myself look and feel better.

I dated a lot and would let the boys do whatever they wanted with me except have intercourse—I could finish that feeling at home. Of course, the guys didn't know that, so I became known as a big tease. Several told me that I drove them crazy for sex, and that made me feel guilty, dirty inside and out, ugly, and a failure again.

Finally the inevitable happened. I did have intercourse with a boy in the front seat of his car outside a drive-in. It wasn't really painful; it wasn't anything. We drove back to his house because his dad was an alcoholic and never at home. We took a shower together, and I did sex dances for him.

When I got home, my stepfather was waiting up for me as he always did. We didn't talk much, just looked at each other, and I went to bed, feeling numb as I fell asleep thinking about all that had happened that night. The next morning I called the boy and told him I never wanted to see him again, and I told everyone at school what a loser he was.

Later I asked my mom if I could wear white to my wedding if I wasn't a virgin. She just said, "You can wear whatever you want." I felt so rejected—I wish she would have asked me what had happened.

After one of our family moves, I rode the bus to my new high school. I had decided I would not make friends with anyone because I hated it there and I hated my stepfather for making us move again. A blonde, bubbly cheerleader got on the bus and sat next to me, holding a trophy and smiling from ear to ear. I just glared at her. I was into cheerleading and pep week at the school I just moved from, and I didn't need her to remind me of what I had left behind.

She talked all the way to school and eventually invited me to her church youth group. I had no idea what a church youth group was, and I certainly wasn't going to make friends with her. However, we rode the bus together for several weeks, and finally I agreed to go.

I was surprised to find a group of kids singing, laughing, and reading Bibles. I remembered how good I felt in church when I was a child, and I felt that way again. My voices told me, *No! These kids won't like you. You are stupid for being here.* But the girl I met on the bus continued to be my friend, and by the end of that school year I asked Christ to come into my life and was baptized.

I was so on fire for the Lord. I had finally found someone who would never leave me, hit me, or make me do bad things—someone who would always love me. I told everyone about Jesus and walked around the house with my Bible, quoting verses. I began a Bible study with my brothers, and we would pray together and talk about Christ's love.

When I was in my senior year of high school, my mom and stepfather had a very violent fight. I was frozen with fear. I couldn't stand to see what had happened with my birth father reenacted, so I took all the money I could find in the house and ran away. I drove to another state and moved in with a boy I had met earlier. The voices in me started up again, saying, *You slut! You call yourself a Christian!*

After a while, my boyfriend and I broke up and I went back home, but my stepfather didn't want me to stay. One night I attended a ball game at a local Bible college. Through all that had been happening, I wore a facade and told people that I was a Christian and that God is great.

However, during the game, I was thinking about my situation: I had been living with a guy, I had come back from running away, and now I had no place to live. Just then, a girl next to me asked if I needed a place to live. I asked if she could read my mind and told her that I did. I moved in with her and two other girls and found out that she was a lesbian and thought I was cute. But that was one relationship I never did pursue.

One of the girls I lived with had a brother I liked, but she was trying to guard his innocence and really didn't want me to date him. However, we started to go out together, and it was a different relationship than I'd ever had before. I knew Jim cared about me—really cared!

Shortly after we were engaged, I cheated on him. I felt so guilty that I gave back the engagement ring, but he wouldn't break off the relationship. I was all mixed up, still masturbating and not eating well. In my heart I wanted him to love me and stay with me, but I was mean to him.

I decided that the man I would marry would have to know the truth about me, so I shared my past with him. He had come from a very strict, sheltered Christian home, and some of the things in my life were hard for him to take, but he told me he loved me anyway. Seven months later we were married.

We never slept together before we were married, but afterward we had a very abnormal sexual relationship. I was addicted to sex, not only with my husband but also with masturbation. This created tension, so we fought, and I began to feel dirty and alone again.

Our first ten years of marriage were turbulent. Jim attended Bible college, worked for a major company for seven years, and then officially went into ministry. I was excited to be a minister's wife and put high expectations on myself to be perfect and always available to help others.

We had two children, but I wasn't much of a mom. I hit them a lot and was easily depressed. I felt like my life was a waste; suicide was a daily thought. I alternated between fits of rage and asking forgiveness. I wanted to be close to God but never felt that I was.

When I became pregnant a third time, a big part of me wanted to have an abortion, but a small part of me said, *Love this child.* My husband was excited about that pregnancy, but we fought even more, and my mood swings went out of control. The baby came, and I didn't know how I could possibly take care of another child. All I wanted was to be out of this life. I was depressed and bored, and I felt ugly and stupid, unwanted and lonely.

Meanwhile, at church and in meetings everyone seemed to like me. I was usually the life of the party, but that was a cover. No one really knew me.

I came very close to having an affair with one of the deacons who was married to my best friend. We never got beyond the talk stage, but I was very tempted and so confused. A voice inside me said, *Go for it. No one will ever know.* But another part of me said, *Be faithful to your husband.* After that I became disinterested in sex with Jim but still had the problem with masturbation.

My stepfather died, and we brought his favorite chair home. When I sat in the chair and looked down our hallway, I could see shadows darting from the kids' rooms to the bedroom across the hall. At first I thought I was just tired, but then I learned that my husband and others saw them too.

One night a figure stood at the end of my bed and stared at me. It was tall and dark with a short-looking child standing beside it. These apparitions occurred off and on for several months. I got more and more depressed and tried to kill myself several times with pills. I talked about death and sang songs about dying. I told my husband that was the only way I would ever have peace—then things would be quiet and I would be with God.

As I became increasingly morose, Jim began staying away at night and would take the kids away for the weekend. He didn't know what to do, so he ran and hid from it all. I would stay in bed for two or three days at a time with the door locked and a sign on the door telling everyone to go away. Meanwhile, Jim would make excuses for me at church, telling everyone I was sick.

Several times our oldest child called for an ambulance, thinking I was dying. They would take me to the emergency room, run some tests, tell me I was fine, and send me home again. Once a minister's name came to mind, and I cried out in desperation for someone to get him to help me. Jim wasn't home, but our babysitter was there, and she called him. He prayed with me and referred me to a Christian counselor, whom I saw for three months.

The counselor began by saying that I was a Christian and he was a Christian but that this was not a spiritual problem. He said I had been abused by several men in my life, I was too busy, and I wasn't facing the child inside me. A small voice inside me said, *But where is Christ in all this?* I knew the answers must be in Him, but I just couldn't get there. I finally stopped going to the counselor.

One day I decided it was time for action, so I took my stepfather's chair to a flea market and sold it. After that, we all stopped seeing ghosts in our home. I quit my job because I had been seeing ghosts there too. At this point I started having a daily Bible study.

Jim and I started to get along better and things became nearer to normal, though I still really wanted to die so he could find a better wife and our kids could have a good mom who didn't cringe when they said, "I love you, Mom." Then Jim was offered another job, and we moved, desperately hoping this fresh start would help us.

In our new location, one of our children began seeing things and having terrible dreams. He wouldn't be left alone. He would see a blond man run through his room and out the door. One night when he was four, he said, "I need the Lord to live in me." He asked Christ into his life and not only did the apparitions and dreams go away, he was also instantly healed of serious asthma attacks and went off all of his medicine and a breathing machine! If you ask him about that today, he will say, "God healed me."

After that brief time of near normalcy, the new job turned into a disaster. I once again started masturbating, fighting, and lying. My husband was fired, and we moved to another location, where God wonderfully provided a home and another job on the staff of a church. With the excitement of the new situation, we were fine for a while, but then depression set in again. I couldn't function, and I just wanted to die. I had no friends; there was no one I could talk to. Who would understand voices, ghosts, deep depression, and an obsession with dying? I lived a double life—trying to help at church, even introducing some to the Lord, while at home I was a hysterical, raging person. I was fooling everyone but my family. I felt as if I were going crazy.

A doctor diagnosed my problem as PMS and said there was a new pill that would help. I believed that a Christian could have physical problems but that my problem was in my mind, and I knew that somehow I needed to end this mental torment.

I was afraid to take a shower for fear that the shower curtain would wrap itself around me and kill me; afraid to answer the phone, not wanting to talk with anyone; afraid to take responsibility, no longer being the person who loved to plan and organize and conduct big events; afraid of the faces in the mirror in my bedroom; and afraid to drive at night because figures and snakes would appear in the headlights.

At a Bible bookstore, I found a prayer notebook, and Jim bought it for me. He was so desperate for me to get better, he would do anything. All through this time, he was telling me that God would bring us through this, he was praying for me constantly, and this time, he wasn't running away to his work.

I brought the prayer binder home and began to have daily morning Bible studies. I had preached to others about having daily Bible study time, but I had never been able to keep it up myself. I began a regular time with God, and it was wonderful. The negative voices stopped, and for a while I stopped masturbating. Prayers were being answered, and our ministry at the church was growing.

In preparation for a Resolving Personal and Spiritual Conflicts conference at our church, a film was shown in which Neil spoke and some people gave testimonies. As I watched, I started getting sick and wanted to run out, but I stayed because of what people would think. On the way home that night I told Jim that I didn't want to go to the conference and that I was better now. I felt that as long as I studied and prayed every morning I would be fine. We talked about it and then dropped the subject. The conference was still two months away, so I felt safe.

The weeks before the conference brought a lot of excitement at church. Everyone was talking about how great it sounded, and they were inviting friends. I decided I would go just to learn how to help others and to support Jim. Then the turmoil started again—I couldn't pray, I became angry easily, and I started masturbating again. I felt so scared and sick that I wished Neil would cancel.

The first night of the conference, I sat there acting cool, taking notes and pretending it didn't affect me. By the third night I couldn't concentrate and nothing made sense. I felt that I would either throw up or dissolve in tears. I heard voices, had terrible thoughts, and was going downhill fast, especially when Neil mentioned rape.

Jim made an appointment for me with Neil, and when he told me about it I started shaking. When the morning of the appointment came, I told Jim there was no way I was going to see some conceited speaker who would just say that I was lying and needed to snap out of it.

Jim prayed a lot and convinced me to go with him to the conference and then to the appointment. That morning I cried through the sessions. Finally, I could take it no longer and went out to sit in the car. This was by far the worst internal struggle of my entire life. I found myself saying, *Why did he come? Doesn't he know that I don't need his help? I like being this way. I'm just fine. Why can't he go away? He will ruin everything.* I especially kept hearing that last thought, *He will ruin everything.*

Then another part of me said, *What could he ruin?* I felt such fear that I thought of driving my car right through the fence in front of me and escaping, but I didn't. I had no place to hide. I wanted help so badly but doubted that Neil would have any answers. Then I got mad. I hated Neil; he was the enemy. I would go to this stupid appointment, but I would win.

Jim found me in the car, and we went to lunch with a friend. Then we went back to the conference, and before I knew it, I was sitting in a room with Neil and a couple from his staff. What happened during the next two hours I will never forget, and I will never be the same.

First I told Neil that I didn't like him and that this wasn't going to work. I told him some of the things about my family in a very matter-of-fact way. I breezed through the first prayer in the Steps to Freedom in Christ with no problem, even though I didn't know what I read. But when it came time to renounce all my cultic, occult, and non-Christian experiences, I couldn't pray. I felt like throwing up, my vision went in and out, and I felt like I was choking and couldn't breathe. I remember Neil quietly telling Satan to release me, affirming that I was a child of God. I felt calmed and continued to go through the prayers.

When we came to the forgiveness part, I told Neil I had no one to forgive, that I loved everyone except him right now. He told me to pray and ask God to bring to mind people I needed to forgive. Names came to mind I hadn't thought about in years. When I started praying to forgive them, I cried and cried, and this time the tears felt good. It felt like a heavy block was being lifted from my chest and head.

We went through the other prayers, and I felt progressively better. I could breathe, and I felt loved. When we had finished, Neil suggested that I go into the restroom and take a good look at myself in the mirror. I did, and for the first time in my life, I liked what I saw! I said, "I like you, Nancy. In fact, I love you." I looked into my eyes and was happy. I felt that because of Jesus, there was a truly good person there. That was the first time I have ever looked in the mirror without feeling disgust for myself.

That night I had to drive three hours to a brother's graduation. Jim couldn't join me because of his responsibilities at the conference.

I had not driven much in the dark because of the images I would see, usually white snakes jumping up at the car. One time I saw a burning car engulfed in flames, but when I got to the spot, nothing was there. I have seen people hitchhiking and then suddenly disappear. So driving at night brought great fear. But that night, during the entire three-hour drive, I saw nothing. Praise God!

The next day, along with 28,000 others, I attended the graduation ceremony. Before this, crowds caused me to panic. I would feel as if I were trapped and couldn't get out, as if I were choking and couldn't breathe, as if the sky were falling around me. That day, however, I felt none of those symptoms. In fact, only when I was walking out of the stadium with people all around me did I finally realize the fear was gone. I looked up at the sky and said, "Praise God, I really am free!"

When I was praying with Neil, what I appreciated most is that it wasn't a typical counseling appointment—it was a time with God. Neil guided me through the prayers and kept me going, but it was God who delivered me from Satan's clutches; it was God who cleaned house in my mind.

The first morning in our home after the conference, I looked around our bedroom and listened. It was quiet, really quiet—no voices, and they haven't come back! Occasionally I have felt frustrated, but now I know how to deal with it.

Since then, our youngest child has had some fears and bad dreams. Instead of praying in fear, we talked about who he is in Christ. Our son said, "Hey! Satan's afraid of me. He had just better watch out 'cause I'm a child of God."

A few months later some missionary friends stayed with us for a week. The wife had been harassed in various ways, including depression and thoughts of suicide. Jim and I led them through the Steps to Freedom in Christ, and they too are free!

Since I found my freedom in Christ, I can say, "I love you" to my husband and not hear thoughts of *No you don't*, or *This marriage will never last*. For a long time now, I have not had depression. I haven't yelled uncontrollably at my children. I'm not afraid of the shower curtain. And masturbation is no longer a problem. Jim and I have been able to lead many of our friends at church through the Steps to Freedom in Christ, and we are enjoying seeing freedom spread. Praise God, I really am free!

Do They Hate You?

You may be wondering why Nancy, Sandy, and others expressed hatred toward me. Obviously, the hatred is not coming from them. Satan isn't pleased with what I'm doing. If we are not experiencing some opposition to what we are doing in ministry, maybe we aren't doing much. If someone expresses hatred when you're trying to help them, just ignore those comments and continue. After they complete the Steps and are free, they are likely to express a great love toward you. Remember Anne's comment in chapter 2? She said, "I immediately had a real love jump in my heart for Neil."

Satan will take advantage of illicit sex more than any other sin that I am aware of. Every sexually abused person I have worked with has had major spiritual difficulties. Compulsive masturbation from the age of three is not normal sexual development, especially for girls. But it is a common stronghold for those who have been sexually violated. These women feel a deep sense of condemnation. They don't have to—there is no condemnation for those who are in Christ Jesus (Romans 8:1).

The stronghold is almost always greater if the sexual abuser is a parent. Parents are the authorities in the home. They are supposed to provide the spiritual protection that children need in order to develop spiritually, socially, mentally, and physically. But instead, abusive parents pass their iniquity on to the next generation. When they become the abusers, they directly open the gates for spiritual assault in their children. Instead of providing a spiritual umbrella of protection, they open the floodgates of devastation.

Guarding What God Entrusts to You

The underlying principle is stewardship. We are to be good stewards of whatever God entrusts to us (1 Corinthians 4:1-2). All parents should know how to dedicate their children to the Lord and pray for their spiritual protection. As parents, we have no greater stewardship than the lives of the children God has entrusted to us.

A Sexual Union and a Spiritual Bond

Every church has a story of a lovely young lady who gets involved with the wrong man. After having sex with him, she can't seem to break away. Friends and family try to convince her that he isn't any good for her. Even she knows the relationship is sick because he treats her like dirt. Why doesn't she just tell him to take a hike? Scripture tells us the reason: They have bonded, or become one in the flesh (1 Corinthians 6:15-17).

A pastor called me one day and said, "If you can't help this young girl I've been counseling, she will be hospitalized in a mental ward." For two years she'd had a sick relationship with a boy who was dealing drugs and treating her as a sex object. The mental assault she was experiencing was so vivid that she couldn't understand why others couldn't hear the voices she was hearing. After hearing her story, I asked her what she would do if I required her to leave this guy and never have anything to do with him again. She started to shake and said, "I would probably get up and leave." From experience, I knew she would respond that way, but I wanted the pastor to hear her response, and I want you to as well. Dissolving that relationship is a worthy goal, but telling her to stop seeing him is not how you get there.

I took her through the Steps to Freedom in Christ. In step 6, she prayed and asked the Lord to reveal to her mind every sexual use of her body as an instrument of unrighteousness, and the Lord did (Romans 6:11-13). As each sexual experience came to her mind, she renounced the use of her body with that person and asked God to break that bond. Her newfound freedom was immediately evident to everyone in that room. Without any coaching, she said she was never going to see that man again, and to my knowledge she never did. That conviction came from the Holy Spirit. Telling our children or friends to break off sexual relationships without resolving the bondage is almost never effective.

God Wants His Children Free

I have found that inquirers need to renounce all sexual sins. I encourage people to pray, asking the Lord to reveal to their minds all the sexual sins they have committed and all the partners they have had, whether they were the victim or the perpetrator. People are amazed at the way experiences come flooding back to their minds. God wants His children free.

When they renounce the experience, they are specifically renouncing Satan, all his works, and all his ways, and they are breaking those ties. When they confess, they are choosing to walk in the light with God. The power of Satan and sin has then been broken, and fellowship with the Lord is beautifully restored.

The Final Word

God wasn't through with Nancy and her husband. Some years later, I received this letter from them.

Dear Neil,

We are full-time missionaries in Africa. We're writing you today because Freedom in Christ Ministries changed our lives many years ago and has continued to be a big part of what we do on the mission field.

Last week we held a camp for 18- to 27-year-olds and took the entire camp through the Steps to Freedom in Christ! It was amazing. Curses were broken, bitterness and hatred toward other tribes were resolved through forgiveness, and blinders were taken off of the students' eyes as they realized who they really are in Christ! Afterward we kept thinking that we would love to share what we are doing with you because you are the one who took us through the Steps years ago and we have been free ever since.

Setting captives free is the main reason why God sent us to Africa. We appreciate your prayers, as you know Africa is a very spiritual place. Daily, we are surrounded by wizards, witchdoctors, and demons, yet we have peace knowing that we are children of the Most High. Life isn't easy out here, but when you know who you are and have been set free from the enemy, you can say, "Greater is He who is in [me] than he who is in the world"!

6

MALE SEXUAL
ABUSE AND FREEDOM

For the healthy Christian, images of sexual perversion are disgusting. Imagine being in full-time ministry and perceiving *yourself* as disgusting. To add insult to injury, what if people rejected you because you were an illegitimate child and because you lived in a racially mixed home?

How would you feel toward yourself? Would you readily accept the fact that you are a saint who sins, or would you see yourself as a wretched sinner? Would you walk in the light, have fellowship with other believers, and speak the truth in love? Or would you live a lonely life in fear, hoping no one would ever find out what your private world is really like? Such is the case in Doug's story.

> My mother wasn't married when I was born, but when I was two years old, she married an Afro-American. He was a decent person, but he never called me his son, and he never said he loved me. Whenever I went somewhere with both of my parents, everyone knew I was not a product of their marriage, and sometimes people called me "Sambo's little kid."
>
> During my preschool years, a babysitter sometimes took me to her apartment and played sexual games with me. In the ensuing years I experimented sexually with other children. I was sexually exploited by older girls and boys, and eventually I was raped by young men.

I thought of myself as a bastard, an unplanned and unwanted accident. Early on I began believing that my craving for love and acceptance might possibly be met through sex, and that by giving fulfillment to others through sex I could show that my love was not selfish. Thus sex became an obsession and eventually led to perversion.

I tried very hard to gain praise and approval in the straight world also, and I won many awards and honors at school. But my self-image was zero, and no person or thing seemed to help. By the time I was 16, I was suicidal.

Then one summer I went to camp and met people who genuinely seemed to care. That was where I learned of Jesus' love for me. The promise of that love, combined with a disgust for myself, drew me to receive Him as my Savior. I then knew that my lifestyle was wrong and that I should turn from it, but I had been programmed to that lifestyle for years and seemed powerless to change.

Nevertheless, I purposed to follow Christ, praying that somehow, by some miracle, I would become the person I longed to be. I trained for the ministry, graduated from school, and threw myself into my work. I think part of my motivation for going into ministry was to give myself to others so they could love me back.

After a few years I married a wonderful woman. Our relationship was doomed from the start because invading thoughts of male images and my own past perversion destroyed any possibility of a healthy sex life. I continually struggled to keep from returning to my former lifestyle. I turned to masturbation, which I considered safe because I could control my environment.

My wife was always loyal to me, yet she sensed something was definitely wrong. Only after we were married for ten years did I finally tell her a little about my problem. That news was very painful for her, but she also felt relieved to finally know the truth.

I heard speaker after speaker talk about victory in Jesus, and I thought, *That's fine for someone who doesn't have my background. That will work for others, but not for me. I will just have to live with my sin. I'll have heaven later, but for now I'll have to deal with the realities of my past.* I felt locked into a horrible identity; it was a heavy bondage.

I developed a contingency plan in the event that anyone ever found out I had been gay or bisexual. I would drive my car into an oncoming truck. I prepared for that through the years by telling people that I would get very sleepy at the wheel and have to eat snacks to stay awake. If I ever committed suicide, I hoped it would look like an accident and my family would receive insurance benefits.

One night in a therapy group, I was hypnotized and told some of my problem—more than I should have. I left with the group's encouragement but did not feel good about what I had shared with them. I looked for approaching trucks on the lonely road home, determined to end my life, but none came along. As I drove into the driveway, my children came running to me. Their acceptance and love were wonderful, and I clicked back into reality.

After some defeats in ministry, I asked for counsel from some older Christian brothers. One of them said, "I hear you saying you are trying very hard to prove you are worthy." That was hard truth, and I immediately began my standard pity party, saying, *Lord, there has never been a person so rejected as me.* Then God seemed to speak aloud to my mind: *The only one I ever turned My back on was My own Son, who bore your sins on the cross.* That was a step toward recovery, of moving away from my prison of self-pity.

Little by little there was growth. God was helping me to see things from a different perspective, and I wasn't so controlled by my passions. But our marriage relationship wasn't all that it should be, and that continued to haunt me.

I had an opportunity to sit under Neil's teaching and heard him speak on spiritual conflict. There I learned some new dimensions of resisting Satan, and on a scale of one to ten, temptations in my thought life went down from a ten to a two. My prayer life became more vibrant and intense. My need for sexual self-gratification diminished until that addiction of a quarter century stopped altogether.

Finally, I found that I could have a normal relationship with my wife without my mind playing a video of others imposing themselves upon me sexually. It was a wholesome, beautiful thing. All of those changes were taking place without my pursuing them. I happened to sit under Neil's teaching, and the Lord did the rest.

Then some difficulties arose, and I realized that I was under attack and needed to go back and reinforce what I had learned. The truth that had helped me in such a variety of ways was the truth of who I am in Christ, defined by my Savior and not by my sin. In Romans, I saw the difference between who I am and my activity: "If I am doing the very thing I do not wish, I am no longer the one doing it, but sin which dwells in me" (7:20). I was finally able to separate the real me from my actions. The reason I was suicidal all those years was that I thought the only way to destroy the sin was to destroy the sinner. There was still an ongoing battle between the authority of my experiences versus the authority of Scripture, but I began to be able to live out my true identity by choosing truth and standing against Satan's lies.

I spoke at a weekend church conference and was able to use the help Neil gave me. After the last session, people began confessing their faults to one another as if we were having a mini-revival. I had never seen anything like it before; it was beautiful to experience.

But even as I spoke at that conference on spiritual conflict, my wife, who was hundreds of miles away, was startled with demonic manifestations in our home. She had to call in friends to support her and pray for her. That became a pattern for a period of time.

We were blessed to minister to people and watch them be set free from bondages that had enslaved them for years. Victims of abuse with dysfunctional relationships were seeing their marriages restored; pastors were being freed from problems paralyzing their ministries. But we also found ourselves harassed by Satan and run ragged by a busy schedule.

As I reflect back to the time when I had planned on taking my life but had come home and met my children in the driveway, I realize that many of my memories from the past had been graciously blocked out. During the demonic oppression that came later, there were flashbacks to perverted behavior and tidal wave after tidal wave of perverse thoughts. Then I would have another onslaught of self-destructive thoughts about suicide being the easiest way to get out of all the pressure we were experiencing.

I went in and out of reality, unable to control it. I became afraid of losing my mind. In the middle of the night, I would awake in a sweat, having dreamed of incredible horror, of killing loved ones and placing their bodies in transparent body bags.

I shared this attack with my brothers in Christ, who offered a massive amount of prayer. I was weak and vulnerable, and I needed the prayer support of God's people to lift that onslaught of demonic depression. Finally it did lift, and I was again able to think objectively and spiritually about the issues.

From experience, I am convinced that no one is ever strong enough to stand alone. I have a wife who prays for me, a support group of men with whom I meet once a week, a Bible study group at church, and concerned friends and loved ones. We all need a body of believers for encouragement, people who will stand with us against the attacks of the enemy.

I'm looking forward to the challenges ahead. Our ministry continues. My wife and I are still working on some issues in our marriage that haven't been totally resolved, but there is nothing there that God cannot heal. My acceptance and identity in Christ are my greatest strengths. Because of His unconditional love, I don't have to prove myself worthy. He has proved His love for me, and I can do nothing to increase that love.

I used to wear the label of bastard, but Colossians explains that in Christ, we are chosen, beloved, and holy. Those are the new labels I now wear, and they are the basis for my true identity in Christ.

When I was a boy and team captains would pick sides for a baseball game, I always seemed to be chosen last. I felt like a handicap to the team who was forced to take me. But God says that He chose me, and not as the last of the group.

Recently I took my dad's hand and told him that I have never loved him more or been more proud of him than I am now. Tears came to his eyes, and he said, "I never knew you cared. I never knew I was that important to you." He reached over and gave me a hug, and for the first time he said, "Son, I love you." How that penetrated the depths of my heart!

God is in the ministry of repairing our lives. He is changing us into His likeness. He is putting all the pieces back together, touching all the relationships between father and son, husband and wife, parent and child. He has begun the good work and will continue it until we stand before Him, complete in Christ.

Where Is Your Identity?

There are a lot of harmful ways to identify ourselves, and doing so by the color of our skin or the stigma connected to our physical birth are two of the sickest. If we had only a physical heritage, we would get our identity from the natural world. But we have a far more important spiritual heritage in Christ.

The apostle Paul repeatedly admonishes the church to put off the old self and put on the new self, "who is being renewed to a true knowledge according to the image of the One who created him—a renewal in which there is no distinction between Greek and Jew, circumcised and uncircumcised, barbarian, Scythian, slave and freeman, but Christ is all, and in all" (Colossians 3:10-11). In other words, our primary identity isn't along racial, religious, cultural, or social lines. We all have a common identity in Christ!

Bondage to Sin

Anybody who would heap more condemnation on this pastor or anyone else who struggles in this way would be assisting the devil, not God. The devil is the adversary; Jesus is our Advocate. People trapped by sexual sin would love nothing more than to be free.

No pastor in his rational mind would throw away his ministry for a one-night stand, and yet many do. Why is that? Can we be bond servants of Christ and at the same time be in bondage to sin? Sadly, many who have been delivered out of the kingdom of darkness and into the kingdom of God's beloved Son are still living in bondage to sin. We are no longer "in the flesh" because we are now alive "in Christ," but we can still choose to walk (live) according to the flesh (see Romans 8:6-10).

Notice that the first deed of the flesh listed in Galatians 5:19 is immorality (fornication). I surveyed a seminary student body and found out that 60 percent were feeling convicted about their sexual morality. (The other 40 percent were probably in various stages of denial.) Every legitimate Christian would love to be sexually free. The problem is that sexual sins are so uniquely resistant to conventional treatment. Nevertheless, freedom is attainable. Let me establish a theological basis for freedom and then suggest some practical steps we need to take. For a more complete understanding, see my book *Winning the Battle Within* (Harvest House, 2008), which deals with freedom from sexual strongholds.

Two Essentials

Two essential issues must be resolved in order for believers to experience freedom in Christ. First, they must break free from the entrapment of sin that resulted when they used their bodies as instruments of unrighteousness. Second, they need to win the battle for their minds by reprogramming them with the truth of God's Word. Paul summarized both in Romans 12:1-2:

> Therefore I urge you, brethren, by the mercies of God, to present your bodies a living and holy sacrifice, acceptable to God, which is your spiritual service of worship. And do not be conformed to this world, but be transformed by the renewing of your mind, that you may prove what the will of God is, that which is good and acceptable and perfect.

In this chapter I will address sexual sin and our physical habits. In the next chapter I will deal with sexual bondage and the battle for our mind.

In Romans 6:12, we are admonished not to let sin reign in our mortal bodies or to obey its lusts. That is our responsibility: to refuse to let sin rule in our members. James warned against "your pleasures that wage war in your members" (4:1).

Dead to Sin

Paul provides a foundational truth that we need to believe in order to prevent sin from reigning in our bodies: "Knowing this, that our old self was crucified with Him, in order that our body of sin might be done away with, so that we would no longer be slaves to sin; for he who has died is freed from sin" (Romans 6:6-7). I often ask participants in a conference, "How many have died with Christ?" Everybody will raise their hands. Then I ask, "How many are free from sin?" According to Scripture, the same hands should be raised.

When we fail in our Christian walk, we will likely be tempted to wonder, *What experience must I have in order for me to live as though I have really died with Christ?* The only experience necessary was the experience that Christ had on the cross. Many try and try to put the old self (man) to death and can't. Why not? Because the old self has already died! You cannot do for yourself what has already been done for you by Christ. Many Christians are desperately trying to become someone they already are. We receive Christ by faith, we walk by faith, we are justified by faith, and we are also sanctified by faith.

We don't always feel dead to sin. In fact, at times we may *feel* very much alive to sin and dead to Christ. But feelings don't always tell the truth. That is why you are to "consider yourselves to be dead to sin, but alive to God in Christ Jesus" (Romans 6:11). Considering this to be so isn't what makes it so. We consider it so because it already is so. Believing something doesn't make it true. It's already true; therefore, we believe it.

When we choose to walk by faith according to what Scripture affirms is true, it works out in our experience, but trying to make it true by our experience will never work. As a believer, you can't die to sin, because you have already died to sin. You choose to believe the truth and live accordingly by faith, and then the truth that you are dead to sin works out in your experience.

Similarly, I don't serve the Lord in order to gain His approval. I am already approved by God; therefore, I serve Him. I don't try to live a righteous life in the hopes that someday He will love me; I live a righteous life because He already loves me. I don't labor in the vineyard in order to gain His acceptance. I am accepted in the Beloved; therefore, I gladly serve Him. What I do does not determine who I am. Who I am determines what I do. So who are you?

Living Free

When sin makes its appeal, I say, *I don't have to sin because I have been delivered out of darkness and I am now alive in Christ. Satan, I have no relationship with you, and I am no longer under your authority.* Sin hasn't died. It's still strong and appealing, but I am no longer under its authority, and I have no relationship to the kingdom of darkness. Romans 8:1-2 helps to clarify the issue: "There is therefore now no condemnation for those who are in Christ Jesus. For the law of the Spirit of life in Christ Jesus has set you free from the law of sin and death."

Is the law of sin and death still operative? Yes, and it applies to everyone who isn't alive in Christ—that is, those who have not received Him into their lives as Lord and Savior. You cannot do away with a law, but you can overcome it by a greater law, which is the "law of the Spirit of life in Christ Jesus." Consider this analogy. We cannot naturally fly because of the law of gravity. But we can fly in an airplane because there is a power there that is greater than the law of gravity. If you think the law of gravity is no longer in effect, cut the airplane's power at 20,000 feet, and you will crash and burn. If you think the law of sin is not still in effect, walk by the flesh. You will crash and burn then too.

The law of sin and death has been superseded by a higher power— the law of life in Christ Jesus. But we will fall the moment we stop walking in the Spirit and living by faith. So we need to "put on the Lord Jesus Christ, and make no provision for the flesh in regard to its lusts" (Romans 13:14). Satan can't do anything about our position in Christ, but if he can get us to believe we aren't in Christ, we will live as though we're not even though we are.

Our Mortal Bodies

In Romans 6:12 we're told to prevent sin from reigning in our mortal bodies, and verse 13 instructs us how to accomplish that: "Do not go on presenting the members of your body to sin as instruments of unrighteousness; but present yourselves to God as those alive from the dead, and your members as instruments of righteousness to God." Our bodies are like instruments or tools that we can use for good or evil. They are not evil, but they are mortal, and whatever is mortal is corruptible.

Christians have the wonderful anticipation of the resurrection, when our bodies will be made imperishable, just like our Lord's (1 Corinthians 15:35-49). Until then, we have mortal bodies that we can use in the service of sin as instruments of unrighteousness or in the service of God as instruments of righteousness.

It is impossible to commit a sexual sin without using our bodies as instruments of unrighteousness. When we do, we allow sin to reign in our mortal bodies. We are being obedient to the lusts of the flesh instead of being obedient to God.

The apostle Paul wrote, "I find then the principle that evil is present in me, the one who wants to do good" (Romans 7:21). Something evil is present in me. It is present in me because at some time I used my body as an instrument of unrighteousness. The passage is not dealing with "the sin principle." The principle is "that evil is present in me." The apostle concludes with the victorious promise that we do not have to remain in that unrighteous state: "Who will set me free from the body of this death? Thanks be to God through Jesus Christ our Lord!" (Romans 7:24-25). Jesus will set us free!

Sinning with Our Bodies

First Corinthians 6:15-20 shows the connection between sexual sin and the use of our bodies:

> Do you not know that your bodies are members of Christ? Shall I then take away the members of Christ and make them members of a prostitute? May it never be! Or do you not know that the one who joins himself to a prostitute is one body with her? For He says, "The two shall become one flesh." But the one who joins himself to the Lord is one spirit with Him. Flee immorality [fornication]. Every other sin that a man commits is outside the body, but the immoral man sins against his own body. Or do you not know that your body is a temple of the Holy Spirit who is in you, whom you have from God, and that you are not your own? For you have been bought with a price: therefore glorify God in your body.

Every believer is alive in Christ and is a member of His body. For me to join my body with a prostitute would be to use my body to sin as opposed to using it as a member of Christ's body, the church. "The body is not for immorality, but for the Lord; and the Lord is for the body" (1 Corinthians 6:13). If you are united to God in Christ, can you imagine the inner turmoil that will result if you are at the same time united physically to a prostitute? That union creates an unholy bond that is in opposition to the spiritual union we have in Christ. The resulting bondage is so great that Paul warns us to flee immorality. Run from it!

Paul puts sexual sins in a category by themselves because every other sin is outside the body. This may have something to do with the ability to create, which we don't have. We can creatively arrange, organize, or otherwise use what God has created, but we don't spontaneously create something out of nothing as only God can do. Procreation is the only creative act that the Creator allows humanity to participate in, and God provides careful instruction as to how we are to oversee the process of bringing life into this world. He confines sex to an intimate act of marriage, requires the marriage bond to last until the death of a spouse, and charges parents to provide a nurturing atmosphere where children can be brought up in the Lord.

Satanic Perversion

Anybody who has helped people who have been victimized in satanic rituals knows how profoundly Satan violates God's standards. These rituals include disgusting sex orgies—not sex as a normal human would understand it, but the most ripping, obscene, violent exploitation of human beings you can imagine. Little children are raped and tortured. The Satanist's ultimate high is to sacrifice an innocent victim at the point of orgasm. The term *sick* doesn't do justice to the abuse. *Total wickedness, utter depravity,* and *absolute evil* better describe this disgusting degradation by Satan and his legions of demons.

Satanists have breeders who are selected for the development of a satanic superrace who, they say, will rule this world. Other breeders are required to bring their offspring or aborted fetuses for sacrifice. Satan will do everything he can to establish his kingdom and to pervert the offspring of God's people. No wonder sexual sins are so repugnant to God. Using our bodies as instruments of unrighteousness permits sin to reign in our mortal bodies. We have been bought with a price, and we are to glorify God in our bodies. In other words, we are to manifest the presence of God in our lives as we bear fruit for His glory.

Homosexual Behavior

Homosexuality is a growing stronghold in our culture, but technically, there is no such thing as a homosexual. Considering oneself to be a homosexual is to believe a lie because God created us male and female. A DNA sample will reveal our true sexual identity. The body is still telling the truth, but our souls have been damaged. Of course, people experience homosexual feelings, tendencies, and behavior, and usually these are developed in early childhood.

Every person I have counseled who struggles with homosexual tendencies has had a major spiritual stronghold. But there is no such thing as a "demon of homosexuality." That kind of thinking would have us believe that if we cast out the demon, the person would be completely delivered from any further thoughts or problems. I know of no such cases, although I would not presume to limit God from performing such a miracle.

The roots of homosexual tendencies usually can be traced to early childhood traumas and sexual abuse. Victims of these tragedies struggle with a lifetime of bad relationships, dysfunctional homes, and role confusions. Their emotions have been tied into their past, and establishing a new identity in Christ takes time. They will typically go through an arduous process of renewing their minds, thoughts, and experiences. As they do, their emotions will eventually conform to the truth they have now come to believe.

Thundering from the pulpit that homosexuals are destined for hell will only drive the people who struggle into greater despair. Overbearing authoritarianism contributes to their demise. Autocratic parents who don't know how to show their love contribute to a child's confused orientation, and condemning messages reinforce an already damaged self-image.

Don't get me wrong. The Scriptures clearly condemn the practice of homosexuality as well as all other forms of fornication. But imagine what it must be like to suffer with homosexual feelings, which you didn't ask for, and then to hear that God condemns you for having them. To deal with this pain, many people want to believe that God created them that way. Militant homosexuals are trying to prove that their lifestyle is a legitimate alternative to heterosexuality, and they violently oppose anyone who would say otherwise.

We must help those who struggle with homosexual tendencies to establish a new identity in Christ. Even secular counselors agree that identity is a critical issue in recovery. How much greater is the Christian's potential to help these people because we have a gospel that sets us free from our past and establishes us alive in Christ! Being a new creation in Christ is what sets us free from our past.

The Path from Sexual Bondage

If you are in sexual bondage, what can you do? First, know that there is no condemnation for those who are in Christ Jesus. Putting yourself or others down is not going to resolve this bondage, and adding shame and guilt will never contribute to good mental health. Accusation is one of Satan's tactics. And most definitely, suicide is never God's means to set you free.

Second, get alone or with a trusted friend, pastor, or counselor and ask the Lord to reveal to your mind every time you used your body as an instrument of unrighteousness, including all sexual sins.

Third, verbally respond to each offense as you recall it by saying, "I confess [whatever the sin was], and I renounce that use of my body." If you have had sexual relationships with others, you also need to ask God to break the bond with that person spiritually, mentally, and emotionally. A pastor told me he spent three hours practicing this by himself one afternoon and was totally cleansed afterward. Temptations still come, but the power has been broken. He is now able to say no to sin. If you think this process might take too long, try not doing it and see how long the rest of your life will seem as you drag on in defeat! Take a day, two days, or a week if necessary.

Fourth, when you have finished confessing and renouncing, express the following: "I now commit myself to the Lord and my body as an instrument of righteousness. I submit my body as a living and holy sacrifice to God. In the name of Jesus, I command you, Satan, to leave my presence." If you are married, also say, "For the purpose of sex, I reserve my body to be used only with my spouse according to 1 Corinthians 7:1-5."

Lastly, choose to believe the truth that you are alive in Christ and dead to sin, and ask the Lord to fill you with His Holy Spirit. Temptation will often seem to be overwhelming, but you must declare your position in Christ at the moment you are first aware of the temptation. Believe with authority that you no longer have to sin because you are a new creation in Christ. Then decide to live by faith according to what God says is true.

Not allowing sin to reign in our mortal bodies is half the battle. Renewing our minds is the other half. Sexual sins and pornographic viewing have a way of staying in the memory bank far longer than other images. I will address that issue after the story in the next chapter.

7

Freeing the Sexual Abuser

Over the phone a pastor asked, "Are you required by law to divulge confidential communication?" In other words, "If I came to see you, could I tell you that I am molesting my child or other children without being turned in to the authorities?" I reminded him that most states still protect clergy confidentiality but do require licensed professionals and public officials, including teachers, to report any suspected abuse. I said that even though I'm not required to do it by the law in our state, I had a moral responsibility to protect another person in danger.

He took the chance and shared his story with me. It all started with rubbing his daughter's back to help her wake up in the morning, but it soon led to inappropriate fondling, though no intercourse was ever attempted. "Neil," he said, "I didn't have a great battle with sexual temptation before this, but as soon as I walk through the door of her room it is as though I have no control." When I talked with his daughter, I understood why.

What was happening reminded me of Homer's depiction of the sirens (sea nymphs) whose singing lured sailors to their death on rocky coasts. Every ship that sailed too close suffered the same disastrous end. In the story, Ulysses ties himself to the mast of the ship and orders the crew to wear earplugs and ignore any pleas he might make. The mental torment of trying to resist the sirens was unbearable.

When we face temptation, a line is drawn. When we step over it, we lose rational control. This pastor crossed that line when he stepped through the door of his daughter's room. As I learned later, the daughter had major spiritual problems that were never resolved. She had been molested by a youth pastor in a former ministry. The daughter wasn't sexually enticing her father, but a demonic stronghold in her life was. The "sirens" lured the father to do the unspeakable. When I met with the daughter, she couldn't even read through a prayer of commitment to stand against Satan and his attacks, which is a definite signal of enemy oppression. The father shared his struggle with his wife, and together, they sought the help they needed.

The story that follows is different from this in at least one respect. Charles's daughter had never been molested, she was never seductive, and she had no apparent demonic stronghold in her life. But at some point in the pursuit of sexual gratification, Charles crossed a line beyond which he lost control. His life became dominated by a power that led him to his daughter's bedroom and caused his world to disintegrate around him. Eventually, he almost lost his life.

Charles is a successful professional who was abused as a child and eventually became an abuser. Thankfully, his story doesn't end there, for after the shipwreck, he experienced a recovery.

> My story is one of God's redemption and the freedom that comes from resting in His grace, a story of being chosen for His work in spite of the opposition of the adversary, Satan. As I write this, I marvel at how little of me and how much of God is revealed in what has happened. I can only praise Him for His transforming work.
>
> I am free from bondage to a vicious assortment of sinful attitudes and habits that cost me the respect of my family, my coworkers, and my church. This bondage put me on a relentless path of personal destruction that, if left unchecked, would have taken my life as well. This freedom was bought at a terrible price that I did not pay. The suffering, death, and resurrection of my Lord Jesus Christ bought my freedom, not my own efforts or my suffering. The life I live is Christ's life, God's Son in me, not my own. And I rejoice that I am able with the help of the Holy Spirit to bring my emotions in line with what I know to be true about myself in Christ. However, this has not happened instantly, and the story of how God molds those He chooses is one of struggle and defeat as well as victory.

"Put down your gun! Don't do it! Jesus, help me! Jesus, help me!" My wife's anguished screams echoed in my ears as I ran for my life while my son loaded his pistol, preparing to hunt me down and kill me. I reached my car in the driveway, fumbled with the keys (*He's coming to shoot me!*), and opened the car door. Throwing my briefcase into the car, I slid behind the wheel and started the engine. I backed out of the driveway and sped down the hill, leaving my wife to struggle with my enraged son, not knowing whether he might shoot her instead, not caring enough to stay and face his wrath.

I raced down the street, imagining my son pursuing me in his car, ready to run me off the road and finish the job. The side streets beckoned as a way to evade pursuit; I made several turns, finally coming to a stop under a grove of trees. My heart was pounding so loud I was sure everyone in the quiet neighborhood could hear it. My shame was so immense, I felt my life was over. I prayed, but all that would come out were groans and hot tears, and they were all for me. I had lost my family in an instant; perhaps my career, my freedom, and my life would follow in rapid succession.

What had happened to me and to my family? What terrible fate had intervened in our affairs, threatening life itself? Where was God when I needed Him most? In my despair I had no answers, just questions and accusations. Thoughts of suicide fleetingly intruded, overcome quickly by my instinct for survival. After the initial fear of pursuit faded, I called a psychiatrist I had just met a couple of weeks before. Tearfully, I explained the situation.

"Do you remember me telling you I felt depressed about my daughter being in the psychiatric ward for the last month?" I began. "She was committed for observation after she ran away and tried to commit suicide. Well, tonight I told my wife why our daughter was depressed. I had sexually molested her. While my wife was still reeling from the revelation, our adult son came in from work, and she told him as he walked through the door. He became like a wild man, striking the walls and calling me a monster. Then he went for his gun, and I ran for my life. When I left, my wife was struggling with him to keep him from shooting me. I don't know what happened after I left." I finished my confession and broke down and wept.

"Find yourself a place to set up housekeeping for a few days while we work this out," my counselor said. "Obviously, you can't go back there just now. And call me when you get settled in so we can talk."

For hours I drove aimlessly, tortured by thoughts of failure, of gross sin, of condemnation and rejection. I felt utterly dejected, despised by everyone—especially by God. I prayed and prayed, but there was no answer. I phoned my supervisor at work, telling him I wouldn't be in until the next day because of a family emergency.

Then I started looking at rock-bottom motels that seemed to fit my current status. Each flea trap reminded me of how low my life had fallen, but my pride kept me from turning in to one of these and registering.

Finally, I settled on a respectable motel, as if to deny the power of the events that had turned my world on its head. The desk clerk asked no questions, but I was sure that disgust must have been lurking behind his calm facade. Once I was inside the room, fear ran through me, unchecked, drenching me with sweat. I had lost my family, my self-respect, and my cockiness, and there was nothing to replace it. I sensed only anger, rejection, and condemnation; there was no hint of hope. I prayed, weeping bitterly over my loss but not facing the sins that led to this moment. I wanted to read my Bible, but I hadn't grabbed it when I fled my home. The motel room didn't have a Gideon Bible, and I didn't think to ask the desk clerk for one.

I slept very little that night. I kept waking, reliving the night before, trying to figure out what I had done wrong and how I could have protected myself better. I was focused on my own feelings of rejection and unworthiness and not on the way I had hurt my family.

What events had led to such feelings of remorse and despair? Nothing mitigates the terrible fact that sin results from the decision to disobey God. We are responsible for our own decisions and actions. Sometimes it's easier to learn from others' mistakes, though. Perhaps some background to my story will help you understand how Satan established beachheads in my life through my responses to life situations.

I was the first child, followed by a brother and two sisters, in a nonreligious family. My parents were married almost 40 years until my father's premature death. Ours appeared to be a traditional family. My father held a succession of occupations, but we didn't move very often, and material needs were always taken care of. In later years, my parents were well-to-do and provided us children with plenty of luxuries. I felt loved and cared for (by the criteria I knew), but I really didn't know much about other kids' home lives, so I didn't make many comparisons. Our family didn't discuss how we got along, how the family was running, or how we responded emotionally to things. My siblings and I didn't discuss our personal lives with one another, much less with the outside world.

In one of my earliest memories, I was spanked for having a toilet-training accident on the bathroom floor. My childish amusement was suddenly transformed into shame, scolding, and physical pain. I didn't know what I had done to call down such wrath; at that young age I was only aware of shame because I had disappointed my mother.

My parents continued to punish and shame me for other accidents, careless or not. Things didn't just happen; someone had to be caught, blamed, shamed, and punished in order for everyone else in the family to feel worthwhile. I only recently learned that this pattern of attitudes had been passed down through both sides of the family for generations.

I was never sure I was valued for being myself. Value seemed to be placed on what I did. Each person in our family constantly jockeyed for position, trying to earn approval or denigrating someone else in order to look better by comparison. At a very early age I started to make choices based on how I would appear to my parents and any other authority figures who were in a position to judge me.

My parents were not religious. My dad, in particular, was actively hostile to all kinds of religion and rarely passed up a chance to make a disparaging remark about those who loved God. We never went to church (I was sent to Sunday school once, but never again), and the Bible was not part of our family.

When I was a teenager, my grandfather gave me a Bible that his mother had given him. It looked new, so my grandfather clearly never read it. He seemed to regard it as a kind of talisman to be passed from one generation to the other, but he never talked about its contents or his relationship to God (if any). So it sat on my shelf next to Bertrand Russell's *Why I Am Not a Christian,* and I got as much use out of it as my grandfather apparently had.

My father often traveled, trying out new businesses in another country and leaving my mother to contend with raising us the best she could. When he was home, he was capricious and wrathful, and the spankings we got were brutal and inappropriate to the offense. There was no warmth at any time, and I remember being told on more than one occasion, "Get out of my sight! You make me sick!" My mother had her own emotional problems with my father, and she was unable to communicate her emotions to anyone, especially her children. So we were on our own, coping in our unique ways with Dad's anger and rejection of us.

When I was about 11, I was introduced to masturbation by a classmate. Confused and fascinated, I found that I could feel better and have pleasure, if only for a few moments at a time. Lacking joy in my relationships, I found myself increasingly drawn to self-gratification as a way of getting solace and comfort when I was lonely or frightened or feeling rejected or inadequate.

My new habit had already begun to isolate me when I discovered the power of fantasy to enhance the experience and heighten the stimulation. I began using the lingerie illustrations in the Sears catalog at my grandmother's house, and I soon found out about pornography through a copy of *Playboy* magazine that my grandmother bought for me (thinking, I suppose, that it had something to do with giving young boys suggestions for play activities). When she saw the contents later that day, she quickly confiscated it, but its contents were already seared into my impressionable mind.

Then I found my father's private stash of hard-core pornography on an upper shelf of his study. He apparently had mail-ordered materials that were illegal at that time (similar items are readily available on the Internet today). I quickly learned to regard women as objects meant to satisfy my lust and stimulate me. Overwhelmed by the boundless promises of lust, I began attempting to make sexual contact with the girls my own age. I was rebuffed, learning very quickly that sexuality was shameful. It was to be hidden, to be snickered at in locker rooms but not to be discussed seriously with anyone.

I was adrift on the sea of lust with no spiritual input and no sense of God's judgment at all. Each episode brought shame that I couldn't talk about with anyone, especially my parents. I felt more and more worthless. I buried myself in academics and became further alienated from my peers.

During all of this, I had the additional misfortune of being seduced by a man I had trusted and liked. He was a prominent authority figure, so I was afraid to tell anyone. Disgusted by the experience and confused by the attention and the sensuality, I felt violated but couldn't admit to my own rage about this until many years later. With my sexuality thoroughly confused, I continued to lust after any sensual experience I could read about or imagine. To satisfy my lust I seduced my younger brother for a period of several years, abusing his natural affections without compassion, pity, or guilt.

I continued to seek out other sensual experiences and pornography. I gravitated toward those that were heterosexual, but the more perversely sexuality was depicted, the more stimulated I became. The transient "adrenaline high" was mixed with shame, the fear of getting caught, and the thrill of avoiding detection. The more I was involved with pornography, the easier I could use it to relieve tension, escape the pressure of social relationships, and avoid unpleasant responsibilities. Pictures on a printed page could promise thrills, ready acceptance, and no conflicts—things that real women and girls my age couldn't offer.

Each time I used the pornography, I was driven into a depression that followed the exhilaration, and I swore that each time would be the last. I reflected on what worthless scum I was. I became more and more isolated from people, rationalizing that if people really knew what I was like, they wouldn't want any part of me.

After I began dating, my primary objective was to get the women I dated to meet my sexual desires. Inflamed with passion by the pornography, I spent hours each day possessed by sexual thoughts and activities, missing assignments because of masturbation, fearful of reaching out socially for fear of rejection, and too stubborn to admit my life was out of control. There were interludes, of course, when my activities were more nearly normal because of involvement with organizations, studies, and occasional friendships. Yet even these were kept away from the core of my being because I was afraid of exposure and rejection.

Gradually I overcame my fear of girls and became preoccupied with seducing them and going as far sexually as I could. As this new outlet for my lust gained proficiency, my abuse of my brother slackened and stopped. I realize now the awful consequences for each of the victims of my lust. I violated them, trespassed their boundaries, and used their bodies without care or respect. At the time, I could only think of more ways to indulge in evil, each thought more perverse and contrary to society's standards than the last. Masturbation became such a preoccupation that my grades suffered and my social relationships eventually dried up. My constant search for stimulating fantasies and experiences hurt other people, invaded their privacy, and drove them away.

When I met my wife-to-be, I was on the rebound from a sexually obsessive relationship that had no solid basis. I knew my new love was a Christian, but I'd had only fleeting contact with "Bible thumpers," as I called them. She was pretty, intelligent, caring, and in need of nurture. Her childhood had been unhappy too.

I thought she would give up Christianity as soon as she learned the truth. She thought I would convert as soon as I heard the gospel.

Neither of us received wise counsel against the relationship, much less the marriage, although we talked to several pastors before getting married. It was a hodgepodge of a ceremony. My bride read from 1 Corinthians 13 and other Scripture passages, but I said nothing religious in my speaking parts and quoted from secular and mystical sources. Significantly, I didn't vow to be faithful or to honor or cherish my wife. At the time, I felt very much in love, but I hadn't the faintest idea about the commitment my bride was making to love me in the love of Christ.

My wife was eager to please her new husband, so initially she satisfied my lust. Even in the marriage bed I considered her just another object placed there for my pleasure to make me feel adequate and loved. I didn't really look very hard for ways to enhance her pleasure other than to order a copy of a Hindu treatise on sex that included hundreds of acrobatic activities that we weren't athletic enough to accomplish (much to my disappointment). I was still looking for the ultimate sexual high the pornography promised but never delivered. Such notions as commitment, nurturing, caring, communication, and fidelity were hard for me to understand.

After our first child was born, we argued bitterly about the religious upbringing of our children. I insisted that they would have none. My wife tearfully shared her fear that they would be condemned to hell if they didn't know Jesus as their Lord. She wanted them to learn about Jesus while they were little. I was adamant that our children not be brainwashed but somehow learn about religion from someone else when they were adults. Although I took a course on the life of Christ and earned an A, I rejected the gospel. I was abusive and hostile, and I angrily blasphemed the living God. My life was in disorder, but I was the last to notice.

Finally, in a time of crisis, having seen many responses to my wife's prayers that I couldn't explain away, I decided to accept the gift of salvation freely offered by the Father through His Son, Jesus Christ. I committed my life to follow Him, having very little idea what that commitment meant. For a time, I was so grateful for having been saved from hell, I set my lust on the back burner. But that didn't last long. I had privately renounced my past sins, but I was unwilling to undergo the self-examination and cleansing that are necessary for a child of God to truly experience the joy of following God in loving obedience.

I heard preachers and commentators refer to God as a loving Father, but that seemed like an oxymoron. I had not experienced such a father. I was expecting punishment, not praise. At the time, I didn't know what God had said about the matter: "Judge nothing before the appointed time; wait till the Lord comes. He will bring to light what is hidden in darkness and will expose the motives of men's hearts. At that time each will receive his praise from God" (1 Corinthians 4:5).

Shortly after I became a Christian, I committed my first act of adultery. I had already had adulterous thoughts, but an opportunity to put my lust into practice presented itself, and I jumped (not fell) into sin. Afterward I was so ashamed that I didn't attempt to continue the relationship. I felt remorse and tried to pray, but I didn't acknowledge to myself or to God my full responsibility in the matter. Three more times over the next several years I took advantage of opportunities to have sex with other women, and my involvement with pornography continued on an episodic basis, adding fuel to the fantasy life that detracted from my relationship with my wife.

Some misguided person might ask if perhaps my wife was unattractive physically or emotionally, implying that somehow she drove me to these sins. I have two responses: First, my wife was (and is) very lovely and was trying to be supportive. Second, I am responsible for my actions regardless of the external circumstances. I focused on sex to meet my emotional needs, and I took that which was not properly mine.

As years passed, my wife began to be troubled by my increasing demands for unusual sex practices, which she considered kinky or perverted. At the same time, my occasional impotence or delay in climax became more frequent. When my wife occasionally tried to talk about these things, I became hostile, defensive, or silent. I was too ashamed of the rest of my sex life to talk about it with anyone, including my wife. If anyone knew about what I was thinking and doing, my life would be over because I was uniquely sinful and worthy of condemnation or death.

I definitely didn't go to God. I believed He accepted only those who were completely obedient to Him, at least in the big things. I knew I was going to heaven, but I believed that God was only keeping a bargain. He couldn't really love me after all the sinful things I had done. I felt out of control, powerless to stop my behavior. I had serious brushes with the authorities, but I didn't stop seeking the magical sexual high that would make me feel loved.

At the same time I pursued those fantasies, I was rejecting any real friendship or intimacy with my wife, with friends, or within Christ's church. I was an elder in our local church, I led home Bible studies, and I even shared the gospel and saw several people accept the salvation of Christ. But inside, I knew no peace.

Some of the pornography I read was "Family Reading," a euphemism for stories about incest. At first the theme seemed repulsive, but then it was stimulating, like other perverted subjects. I didn't apply it to my own family at first. Then, as my daughter reached 14, I began to notice her maturation in an unhealthy way. My language at home became more suggestive, my remarks less appropriate, the jokes I brought home from work more sexual. I was less careful about modesty in my dress. When I saw my daughter in swimwear or nightwear, I struggled to avert my eyes.

Finally, when telling my daughter good night in her bedroom, I would find one pretext or another to "accidentally" brush a hand against her breast, even while praying with her. This happened over a period of several months. I became afraid of what would happen next, but I told myself I couldn't help it and that I really loved my daughter.

My ambivalence interfered with my sex life with my wife, and I found myself increasingly impotent with her. Even masturbation failed to satisfy.

One evening I offered to tell my daughter good night. "No thanks, Daddy, I'm too tired," she said, as she went into her bedroom and firmly closed the door. There were no more good nights after that. She didn't want me to hug her or even touch her, claiming that her muscles were tender from workouts. A gulf grew between us, but in my deception I didn't attribute her rejection of me to the abuse of our relationship, to violating her boundaries as a person, or to my transgressing God's law. I attributed her coldness to growing pains, failing to recognize that I had hurt and frightened her and had perverted our relationship.

Several months later, relationships in our family had deteriorated severely. No one was communicating effectively with anyone else, and we were all barely coping with day-to-day existence. After a thoroughly botched vacation trip, no one talked all the way home, and things became even worse. My wife became severely depressed, entering a psychiatric unit for more than a week. While she was there we were all distraught, yet I did not tell anyone about my secret life, which corrupted everything in our family.

Although I did not abuse our daughter during that tumultuous period, I failed to take decisive action, and she became more depressed than ever. A couple of weeks after my wife returned from the hospital, our daughter ran away. When we finally tracked her down a few days later in a nearby community, she was defiant and didn't want to come back home. One of her acquaintances told us she had narrowly been prevented from committing suicide. So our daughter went into the hospital for a month.

While she was in the hospital, not a hint of the story of her sexual abuse came out until the last week. In spite of repeated questioning by the mental health team and my wife, she denied there was anything between us, and so did I. It was as if we believed we could wish away the incidents, as if nothing had really happened. But it had, and that monstrous sin festered beneath the surface, becoming more foul. There was little progress in our daughter's depression and anger, and daily my wife and I were becoming more distant from one another.

Finally, I woke up at four o'clock one Thursday morning, sitting bolt upright in bed with a compelling urge to confess everything to my wife. Although my intent was to tell everything, my almost-as-great compulsion to protect and defend myself produced a protracted confession lasting four days. There were falsehoods, half-truths, whole truths, all tumbling together with tears and remorse. She heard about the adultery, the incest with my siblings, seduction by the older man, the confrontations with the authorities. And she kept asking about our daughter while I kept denying there was anything amiss.

Finally, on the fourth evening, I told my wife I had abused our daughter. She sat there in stunned silence and horror. "That explains a lot," she finally said. "I couldn't put things together in my mind, but now events make sense." Just then our son walked in, and you know what the rest of that evening was like. A couple of elders from our church came over that night, prayed with my family, encouraged them as much as they could, and offered them help. One of them took the guns from our house. My wife contacted the Child Protection Agency the next day (an essential action, mandated by law when abuse is discovered).

I moved to a less expensive motel for a couple of weeks while my wife decided what to do. I couldn't call the house because my son was there. My days were spent in pain, grieving my losses, berating myself. I found a Bible and began reading verses about those who are in Christ and God's love for us. I cried a lot. I read Psalm 51, King David's confession of sin with Bathsheba, over and over. I prayed aloud to God; I screamed into my pillow and drenched it with tears. I wept over the remains of a wasted life, of broken relationships.

I slowly began to realize how my sins had produced consequences in the lives of others that couldn't be erased. From my motel room, I called our church friends, pouring out my anguish to them. I was amazed that they didn't hang up on me. They didn't approve of my behavior, but they were still talking to me.

I couldn't attend the church my wife and daughter were attending, so I looked in the Yellow Pages for a church close to my motel. I was sure my shame was written all over my face, but I knew I had to be with God's people, even if they threw me out on my face. The first service I attended was about sin and God's mercy. I was blinded with tears, and the lump in my throat kept me from singing.

After the service, I asked the man who had been sitting next to me to recommend a mature Christian I could talk to. Sensing the urgency in my voice, he introduced me to a man about my age who took me outside to talk. Sobbing, I told him the whole story, sparing nothing. "I don't want your church just to accept me as some kind of saint, welcoming me with open arms," I said. "I've hurt a lot of people, and my sin has hurt me as well."

I'll never forget that man's response: "Friend, this church is a place for healing. You are welcome here." Unmerited grace flooded my heart and I wept uncontrollably at his generosity. I had never considered the church to have a ministry to people wounded by their sin. But I returned the next Sunday and took the risk of meeting some of the elders of the church and the pastor and sharing my story with them. I asked for prayer for my family and for me. The response didn't excuse my sin, but it was clear that they considered me a child of God worthy of respect. I was overwhelmed by gratitude.

My wife was grief-stricken, angry, fearful, and depressed over the revelations of my infidelity. In spite of that, she took time to call me at the motel and check on me. She got me the essentials for living out of the house and smuggled them to me. She spent hours in secluded places with me, talking out her frustrations and encouraging me to deal with reality as I confronted my sins.

We had periods when emotions were so high we didn't talk to one another for days at a time, but God always brought us back to each other.

One of our friends from our old church recommended a Christian counselor he had known for years. "He's a gentle man, full of wisdom, and I've heard that everything he tells you he backs up with scriptural truths so you can check it out." Although I was seeing a secular psychiatrist, we decided to go to this man for help.

He listened to the whole sordid story and said, "There are major problems here, but none that God can't handle." He began to teach us to communicate the feelings in our hearts with one another without killing one another's spirits in the process. He taught us the basis for sin and our reaction to it, beginning with Adam and Eve in the Garden of Eden and working from there through the Bible. We began to see hope.

In addition to the counseling sessions, our counselor recommended several books to read as we went along. One book he recommended was *Victory over the Darkness*. For the first time, I began to understand that because I am in Christ, certain things are true about me that are also true of Christ.

Because of my identity in Christ, I have power over the things in my life that I always assumed were beyond my control. In particular, I learned that my emotions and my actions are governed by what I think and believe and especially by who I believe myself to be. If I believe a lie about my essential nature, whether it is from the world, the flesh, or the devil, I will act according to that belief. Similarly, if I choose to believe what God has said about me, I will govern my thoughts and my actions that proceed from those thoughts in accordance with God's will.

I experienced a dramatic sense of joy and freedom when I realized that God will always love me completely, regardless of the particulars of my sin. It was a profound revelation to see from the Scriptures that I am not just a sinner saved by grace, but a saint who sins, one who is called out and sanctified by God. I learned from our counselor how to appropriate the truth that I have an advocate before the Father who is constantly there to counter Satan's charges against God's elect. I began to experience periods of real joy for the first time, interspersed with periods of melancholy and deep, abiding sorrow before God for my sins against Him and against other people, particularly my daughter and my wife.

I continued to hate myself until my wife reminded me, "You need to remember that if God has forgiven your sins in Christ, you must now forgive yourself." I have had to work to forgive those who hurt me in the past, not because those hurts are an excuse for sins old or new, but because the unforgiveness kept me bottled up. I have asked for and received forgiveness from family members I hurt (with the exception of my children, who are still struggling with it), and I have been reconciled to them, knowing true intimacy for the first time in my life with my brother and sisters and mother. My father died as an unbeliever a number of years ago, rejecting the gospel till the last. Forgiving him for the rage and neglect has been hardest, but God has called me to that as well.

I had been attending two different 12-step groups for sexual addiction, but I quit when I realized that sexual sobriety was their only goal.

Although they acknowledged a Higher Authority, they weren't permitted to identify that Authority as Jesus Christ. When they had a split vote on whether sex was permitted only in marriage or just in a committed relationship, whether homosexual or heterosexual, I realized I was in the wrong place and left the groups for good.

Still, those groups opened my eyes to the sexual dysfunction in our society. There are plenty of people out there involved in sexual sin. But these groups could not offer the spiritual perspective that identified the life-changing power of Jesus Christ inside the hearts of those who trust and obey Him. Because of that, I am hesitant to recommend their self-help approach, particularly if it detracts from relationships in the body of Christ. These groups often claim in meetings that the addicts are the only ones who can understand one another, that they are the addict's true family. To a Christian, such an attitude misses the point of the body of Christ caring for its members who are hurting.

I read another book that shed tremendous light and gave me hope and direction—*The Bondage Breaker.* I learned that we enable Satan and his unholy angels to establish footholds and then strongholds in our spiritual lives when we don't live in our identity with Christ and appropriate the aspects of His character that are already ours. The book gave hope for victory in the spiritual and physical struggle over sin by reminding me that Satan is a vanquished foe who has no power over me unless I relinquish it to him.

I began to read aloud from both books, emphasizing the spiritual truths that show our identity in Christ and the results of that identity. As I affirmed my identity and then struggled with the discrepancy between my current experience—my attitudes, thought life, and behavior—and my nature in Christ, I was often overwhelmed with grief and self-condemnation. I renounced the strongholds Satan had established, and I experienced progressive freedom as I identified each troubled area. After months of struggle, I am finally on the path God has for me: confident in Him, not in myself, and confident in His love for me, which will not fade or fail.

My wife and I have worked for the last year toward reestablishing our relationship, based not on lust and exploitation but on the solid foundation of Jesus Christ. Gradually, we have dealt with issues of sin and forgiveness, and we are friends again. We still have arguments, conflicts, and hurt feelings to deal with, but our tools are better. We are build-ing a track record of success in resolving our past and present conflicts.

I still struggle with my emotions, but I am able to feel the full range from profound sadness to great joy, and God is with me in all of them. Do I still sin? Surely, but I am a saint who sins, and I am able to confess to God, remembering I John 1:9 (NIV): "If we confess our sins, he is faithful and just and will forgive us our sins and purify us from all unrigh-teousness." And I have been wonderfully freed from the sexual com-pulsion that grew out of believing Satan's lies about my true nature.

With the help of my therapist, I have been learning to recognize and acknowledge my emotions. The Holy Spirit empowers me to do good rather than evil. I have not been magically freed from temptation; as I draw closer to God, the tempter presents more opportunities for sin. Recognizing that my thoughts will bear fruit if they are allowed to, I am constantly making choices for what is right. The bondage to sin that I allowed to happen through my sinful choices has been broken. In the midst of the evil around me, I am learning to flee temptation, resist the devil, and be in the world but not of it. I stand on God's promise: "No temptation has seized you except what is common to man. And God is faithful; he will not let you be tempted beyond what you can bear. But when you are tempted, he will also provide a way out so that you can stand up under it (I Corinthians 10:13 NIV).

I am confident that God's timing and His methods are perfect, that His plan of redemption has no flaws. I am grateful for His restoration, and I look forward to the time when all wounds are healed, all tears are wiped away, and reconciliation in Christ is perfected. Until then, I am learning how to take responsibility for my actions and to love my wife the way God intended. Now I am able to pray, to study Scripture with gratitude, to praise God for His grace, and to rest in His provision for my life. Now that I understand my identity in Christ, I am free! I can live the life God calls me to live!

Five years after our first meeting, I accidentally met this couple again in a restaurant. They wanted to tell me about the class on marriage they were teaching in their church. I hesitated at first to ask how the children were doing, but I finally did. "Oh, we are all reconciled, and our son is going into full-time ministry." Talk about the power of God to transform lives!

Who Are the Hurting?

When I was on the faculty at Talbot School of Theology, I taught a required ethics class that examined the church's role in society. During the semester, we invited local experts to address specific moral issues. I enjoyed the class because every spring it provided a learning experience for me as well. As the guests came to give their presentations, I warned the students not to "pick up everybody's burden," or they would be overwhelmed. However, I wanted them to sense each presenter's passion because each one was called by God to meet specific needs of hurting people in our society. That is the calling of the church.

Parachurch ministers often tell me about their frustration with the church. Many think the church is living in denial and even providing a safe haven for wife beaters, child abusers, and alcoholics. Churches fail to defend victims and provide sanctuary for abusers in order to avoid scandals. Consequently, neither abusers nor victims get help. That is not totally true of course, but it does happen all too often.

Male and Female Sexuality

We are created as sexual beings: Female vaginal lubrication and male erections take place in the first 24 hours after birth. Infants need to experience warmth and touch in order for parental bonding to take place, and trust is developed during the first few months of life. Abuse or neglect during this early time will have lasting detrimental effects. No wonder children are hurt so severely if they are abused later in early childhood, when there is even greater awareness.

All sexual anatomy is present at birth and develops in early adolescence. Hormones start secreting three years before puberty. In the female, estrogen and progesterone are very irregular until a year after puberty, when a regular rhythmic monthly pattern is established. The wall of the vagina thins and vaginal lubrication decreases after menopause as hormone secretion decreases.

In the male, testosterone increases at puberty, reaches a maximum at 20, decreases at 40, and is nearly gone at 80. Normal aging causes a slower erection and less sexual functioning but not a complete stopping of those functions. While a man is sleeping, he will have an erection every 80 to 90 minutes.

All this is a part of God's wonderful creation, which we are to watch over as good stewards. However, this beautiful plan for procreation and expression of love can be grossly distorted.

Healing a Distorted Sexual Development

God intended sex to be for pleasure and procreation within the boundaries of marriage. But when sex becomes a god, it is ugly, boring, and enslaving. We cannot free the captives by heaping condemnation on them. Increasing shame and guilt is counterproductive and will not produce good mental health, Christian character, or self-control. Guilt does not inhibit sexual arousal. It may even contribute to it and keep us from using our sexuality wholesomely as God intends. Instead of condemning those who have had a distorted sexual development, consider offering the following six steps to them.

1. Seek resolution for all personal and spiritual conflicts. People don't have a sex problem, a drug problem, or an alcohol problem. They have a life problem that can be resolved only when they are fully reconciled to God. There are no secrets with God. He knows the thoughts and intentions of our hearts (Hebrews 4:11-13). We don't have to fear rejection when we are totally honest with Him. To make confession is to live in conscious moral agreement with God, knowing that we are already forgiven. The opposite of confession is not silence, but rationalization and self-justification. When the barriers to our intimacy with God are removed, the grace of God works in our lives, moving us toward wholeness. That is what we are trying to accomplish with the Steps to Freedom in Christ.

2. Commit yourself to a biblical view of sex and live accordingly. All sexual expressions were intended by God to be associated with love and trust, which are necessary to ensure healthy sexual functioning. Recent evidence indicates that trust may be one of the most important factors determining orgasmic capacity in women. People can trust us when they know we will never violate their conscience. In other words, if it is wrong for your spouse, it is wrong for you.

Too many wives have tearfully asked me if they have to submit to their husband's every request. Usually their husbands are asking for something kinky, hoping to satisfy their lust. Some of these men actually appeal to Hebrews 13:4, saying "the wedding bed is to be undefiled" and claiming that the Bible permits all expressions of sex in a marriage. No seven words are taken out of context more than those. The verse continues, "for fornicators and adulterers God will judge." The idea is to never let the wedding bed be defiled by adultery or fornication.

A wife can meet the sexual needs of her husband, but she will never be able to satisfy his lust.

A biblical view of sex is always personal. It is an intimate expression of two people who are in love with each other. People who are in bondage to sex or are bored with it have depersonalized it. They become obsessed with sexual thoughts in hope for more excitement, and because obsessional sex is always depersonalized, boredom increases and obsessive thoughts grow stronger. One man actually told me that his practice of masturbation is not sinful because in his fantasies, the women have no heads! I told him that is precisely what is wrong with what he is doing. He sees people as sex objects, not as people created in the image of God. Even the porn queen is some mother's daughter and not just a piece of meat.

Biblical sex is also safe and secure. Outside of God's plan, fear and danger can also cause sexual arousal. For instance, sneaking into a porn shop will cause sexual arousal long before an actual sexual stimulant is present. And voyeurism is resistant to treatment because arousal is not just from the viewing—the excitement comes from violating a forbidden cultural standard. The emotional peak is heightened by the presence of fear and danger.

One man said he was into "exciting sex." He would rent a motel room and commit adultery in the swimming pool, where the possibility of being caught heightened the climax. Such people must separate fear and danger from sexual arousal. A biblical view of sex is associated with safety and security, so maximum fulfillment comes from a complete surrender of oneself to another in trust and love. Some people buy the lie that the forbidden fruit is the sweetest, denying the crucial importance of the relationship between a man and a woman in finding pleasure and fulfillment in sex.

We should also abstain from any use of the sex organs other than that which the Creator intended. I was not built upside down or intended to walk on my hands. Parts of my body are created to dispose of unusable body fluids and substances. I do not believe oral sex reflects the Creator's design for proper use of body parts, and one does not need to have someone from the opposite sex to participate. Even personal hygiene would suggest that this expression isn't what God intended.

Why are we continually looking for the ultimate sexual experience?

Why aren't we looking for the ultimate personal experience with God and each other, and letting sex within marriage be an expression of that? Good sex will not make a good marriage, but a good marriage will have good sex.

3. *Seek forgiveness from all those you have sexually offended.* I encourage every man to go to his wife and ask for forgiveness for any violation of trust. Our wives can sense when something is wrong; don't force them to make guesses about the problem. Wives play a critical role in helping their husbands live sexually free in Christ. Men are more vulnerable sexually, and they need the caring support and discernment that a loving wife can provide. Both Doug (from our last chapter) and Charles finally confessed everything to their wives. Humbling? Yes, but that is the path to freedom.

Charles also had to seek forgiveness from his children. In some cases, children may be able to forgive only after years have passed. Sadly, some never come to the point of forgiving their abusers, so the cycle of abuse continues. Abused children usually become abusive themselves, and their children will suffer the result of yet another parent in bondage. If the victim chooses not to forgive the abuser, he or she is living in the bondage of bitterness. Yet for the restored abuser to live in condemnation because he or she has not been forgiven by the victim is to deny the finished work of Christ. Christ died once for all for the sins of the world. We must believe, live, and teach these truths in order to stop the cycle of abuse. We all have the privilege of throwing ourselves on the mercy of God.

4. *Renew your mind.* Abnormal sex is a product of obsessive thoughts. These thoughts and the actions they lead to reinforce themselves and are therefore self-perpetuating. The mind can reflect only on that which is seen, stored, or vividly imagined, and we are responsible for what we think and for our own mental purity.

When I first became a Christian, I committed myself to clean up my mind. As you undoubtedly can guess, the problem became worse, not better. If you are giving in to sexual thoughts, temptation doesn't seem that strong, but when you determine not to sin, temptation becomes stronger. I remember singing songs just to keep my mind focused. My life and experiences are quite innocent compared to the experience of most people I have talked to, but nonetheless, the process of renewing my mind from the images I had programmed into it earlier took a long time.

Imagine your mind to be the liquid in an ignored coffeepot. The fluid is dark and smelly because of the old coffee grounds (pornographic material and sexual experiences) that have been left in it. There is no way to rid the bitter taste and ugly coloring that now permeate it, no way to filter it. You can and must get rid of the grounds. All pornographic material must go!

Now imagine a bucket of crystal-clear ice (representing the Word of God) alongside the coffeepot. If you were to take at least one ice cube every day and put it into the coffeepot, the coffee would eventually be watered down so much that you couldn't smell or see the coffee that was originally there. That process will work as long as you are not putting in one ice cube *and* one pornographic image each day as well.

Paul writes in Colossians 3:15, "Let the peace of Christ rule in your hearts, to which indeed you were called in one body; and be thankful." How are we going to let Christ rule in our hearts? The next verse says, "Let the word of Christ richly dwell within you, with all wisdom teaching and admonishing one another with psalms and hymns and spiritual songs, singing with thankfulness in your hearts to God."

As Jesus modeled, we must stand against temptation with the truth of God's Word. When a tempting thought first hits, take it captive to the obedience of Christ (2 Corinthians 10:5). "How can a young man keep his way pure? By keeping it according to Your word…Your word I have treasured in my heart, that I may not sin against You" (Psalm 119:9,11). Winning the battle for our minds is often two steps forward and one step back. Eventually, it is three steps forward and one back. Then it's five steps forward and one back, and someday there are so many positive steps forward that the one step back is a fading memory. Remember, you may despair in confessing when you fall again and again, but God never despairs in forgiving.

5. Seek legitimate relationships that meet your authentic need for love and acceptance. People with sexual addictions tend to isolate themselves. We need each other; we were never designed to survive alone. Charles sought out Christian help and fellowship. Few do that, however, because of the shame. Consequently, they stay in bondage. When we are satisfied in our relationships, deep legitimate needs are met. Finding fulfillment in sexual expressions instead of relationships will lead to addiction.

6. Learn to walk by the Spirit. Galatians 5:16 says, "Walk by the Spirit, and you will not carry out the desire of the flesh." A legalistic walk with God will bring only condemnation, but a dependent relationship with Him, with His grace sustaining us, is our real hope.

Admittedly, overcoming sexual bondage is difficult, and that is why we need the grace of God. The terrible cost of not fighting for that freedom is too high a price to pay. Your sexual freedom is worth the fight.

There is another chapter in Charles's story. After I spoke at the biannual meeting of the American Association for Christian Counseling, Charles's son came up and introduced himself. In the course of our conversation, I said, "I heard that you were called into full-time Christian ministry." He affirmed that he was now working with a recovery ministry for the abused. The old cycle of abuse has been replaced by a new cycle of reconciliation. Praise God!

8

MINISTERING FREEDOM TO THE HISPANIC CHURCH

I have been privileged to speak in most of the Latin American countries. Christianity is somewhat on the decline in the United States, but that is not the case in Spanish speaking countries and communities. A couple approached me when I was on a mission trip to Romania. They were missionaries from El Salvador, and they were in Romania to share the message of Freedom in Christ. Representatives from Venezuela were doing the same in Sweden. Most of my books have been translated into Spanish, and our ministry has representatives throughout Latin America.

The best examples of churches using our material come from the Casa Sobre la Roca churches in Bogota, Colombia. Pastor Dario Silva-Silva was an award-winning political correspondent in Colombia when he came to Christ. He was introduced in those early years to our message and decided that would be the core message of his church. I spoke at the tenth anniversary of his home church. At the time they had 3000 members and had started seven other churches. All new Christians and new members are led through our discipleship course and the Steps to Freedom in Christ. Then they are baptized and brought into the church. That is the same order that the early church practiced—a rite of exorcism preceded the rite of baptism.

I spoke again at the twentieth anniversary of this church and conducted Discipleship Counseling conferences in five different cities in

Colombia. They now have more than 30 churches, and they are the most disciplined and healthy churches that I have had the privilege to address. Colombians Glen and Katy Arias have joined our staff in the United States. They found their identity and freedom in Christ while attending a Casa Sobre la Roca church in Colombia, and they will share a little of their story at the end of this chapter. But first, let's hear from pastor César Buitrago, who is from El Salvador but now lives in California.

A Young Believer

"There are many young people here who are old inside. There are no visible wrinkles on their faces, but their souls are aching." The priest was addressing dozens of young students from my Catholic school in El Salvador while we were at a camp. I felt as though the message was directed to me. The priest continued, "Just like Nicodemus, you must be born again, and only Jesus can make you a new person from the inside out."

As I left the camp, the Word of God continued to pierce me. I fully identified with Nicodemus. I had years of religious training and knew a lot about God, but I did not know Him personally. When I got home, I knelt down by my bed and prayed: *Jesus, if what the priest said is true—that You are the only one who can make us new—would You please come into my heart and become my Savior? I want to be a new person.*

That was the beginning of a new and exciting life with Jesus Christ. I was only 16 years old at the time. The first sign that I was alive in Christ was my hunger for His Word. I read and reread the Bible and sought to apply it to my life on a daily basis. I also had a deep desire for spiritual community and accountability. The Lord led me to regularly meet with other believers for prayer and encouragement. The third sign was a passion to share Christ with others. Dozens became followers of Christ as they listened about my newfound friend!

Like most Latinos, I had believed in God and knew about Him, but what a difference when God revealed Himself to me and I got to know Him personally! When we seek God, He will make Himself known to us, and our lives will never be the same.

A New Identity

A few years later, the Lord called our family out of our war-torn country of El Salvador, and we moved to San Jose, California, where He led me to plant a Latino church. During those early years as a young pastor, I discovered Freedom in Christ Ministries and learned about my identity in Christ. We were greatly encouraged by the clear and relevant biblical message Neil was sharing with the body of Christ through his books and conferences. Understanding the truth about God's unconditional love gave us a sense of security and significance.

Most Latinos come from a strong religious background that emphasizes works. We tend to focus on what we can do for God. This focus keeps us in a constant state of insecurity about our relationship with Him because we are never good enough. Consequently, we keep trying harder and continue in a vicious religious cycle. We try to keep His commandments, but lacking an understanding of the life of Christ in us, we are not able to do it. Praise the Lord for the liberating truth that we are already complete, secure, and significant in Christ, and it's all because of what He has done!

Most Pauline epistles begin with the recognition and affirmation of our identity in Christ. The book of Ephesians is a great example:

> Praise be to the God and Father of our Lord Jesus Christ, who has blessed us in the heavenly realms with every spiritual blessing in Christ. For he chose us in him before the creation of the world to be holy and blameless in his sight. In love he predestined us to be adopted as his sons through Jesus Christ, in accordance with his pleasure and will—to the praise of his glorious grace, which he has freely given us in the One he loves...

> You also were included in Christ when you heard the word of truth, the gospel of your salvation. Having believed, you were marked in him with a seal, the promised Holy Spirit (1:3-6,13 NIV).

Notice Paul's emphasis on what God has already accomplished on our behalf through Jesus Christ. This is indeed a cause for great rejoicing and praise to our heavenly Father! In these verses Paul reminds us who we are. We were chosen by the Father, redeemed by Jesus Christ, and sealed by the Holy Spirit. Because of His love, we have been forgiven, accepted, bought back, adopted, regenerated by the Spirit, and set apart for God. We are His children, and nothing can separate us from His love!

Consider this illustration. A farmer took an eagle's egg from a nest just a few hours before it was hatched and put it by chicken eggs. The little eagle was born among chickens. He learned to think like a chicken, eat like a chicken, behave like a chicken, and live like a chicken. One day the little eagle saw a majestic bird flying high in the sky and asked one of his fellow chickens, "Who's that?"

"That's an eagle," the chicken replied. "He is the king of all birds, but you will never be able to fly like him!"

On another day, the eagle flew to the farm and confronted the little eagle. "What are you doing here? You are an eagle!"

The young eagle who thought he was a chicken was surprised by this revelation. Eventually he accepted the truth that he was indeed an eagle, and with a little help from the older eagle, he learned to fly and live like one!

Too many Christians are like this eagle. They are living below their privileged position. They have all they need to live victorious Christian lives, but they live as though they were still the same people they were before Christ gave them new life. So they walk like chickens when they could soar like eagles and overcome the temptations of this world. Knowing who we are in Christ is critical to our spiritual health and growth as believers.

This message is desperately needed in the Latino church. Without it we will gravitate toward our religious traditions and will most likely miss the opportunity to experience the victorious life God designed for us! An estimated 12 million Latino Christians live in the United States and comprise the largest minority group. Imagine the impact these believers would have in their respective countries if they were established alive and free in Christ.

Connecting to God

Most Latinos were baptized when they were infants and never fully embraced their faith. They believe in God and fear His punishment, not knowing that the punishment we deserved has already fallen on Christ. "There is no fear in love; but perfect love casts out fear, because fear has to do with punishment. The one who fears is not made perfect in love" (1 John 4:18 NIV). They also believe in Jesus, who died for their sins. Many believe He is still on the cross and is not functionally relevant to our daily living. They need to embrace the whole gospel. Jesus didn't only die for our sins, He also destroyed the works of Satan and was resurrected to give us new life. Not realizing the spiritual battle they are in, many Latinos embrace cultic and occult practices, such as Santeria, witchcraft, and fortune-telling. Syncretism is a major problem crippling the Latino church.

Most Hispanic pastors are committed to seeing people's lives transformed. Unfortunately, few pastors and leaders are equipped to help new believers deal with the spiritual bondage plaguing them. A few years ago my wife and I were counseling a young lady who was struggling with guilt. She had aborted a child and was not able to forgive herself for such a horrible sin. We shared with her that Jesus had already died on the cross for her sins and was resurrected so that she could have a new life in Him. This satisfied God's justice and demonstrated His incredible love for us!

When she understood and chose to believe in the finished work of Christ, she confessed her sin to God and received His forgiveness. We could see the joy on her face! She had dealt with one of the most painful experiences in her life. She then decided to get baptized and continued experiencing the joy of 1 John 1:8-9 (NIV): "If we claim to be without sin, we deceive ourselves and the truth is not in us. If we confess our sins, he is faithful and just and will forgive us our sins and purify us from all unrighteousness."

Christ's Power to Set Us Free

I soon discovered that this young lady's experience was typical. Most of the Christians in our church were struggling with unresolved personal and spiritual conflicts and were struggling with resentment, bitterness, pride, lack of forgiveness, family trauma, every kind of abuse, and poverty. They loved the Lord and believed in Him, but they struggled with spiritual bondage, which blocked the process of sanctification.

Frustrated by lack of growth in our people and lacking the tools to help them, I attended a Freedom in Christ symposium and became familiar with the Steps to Freedom in Christ. I set up a process to lead our people through them. We learned how practical and thorough they were, and we glorified our Lord Jesus Christ as He manifested His presence and set captives free. We began to use the Steps with those who were preparing for baptism and saw great fruit in their lives as a result of the freedom they were experiencing.

Hundreds of believers were set free from witchcraft, Santeria, sexual addictions, and traumas precipitated by emotional and physical abuse. Relationships were deeply healed as people learned to forgive, and entire families were completely restored by the grace of God. Our church was revitalized by the Holy Spirit as people experienced a new sense of purpose and fulfillment.

We began by prayerfully selecting 20 servant leaders who would eventually help others. We asked them to commit themselves to three hours of training each week and invited them to go through the Steps. Those who did were invited to participate in the training to help others. The group kept growing, and we saw many people experience the liberating power of Christ.

I have learned several principles while taking people through the Steps to Freedom in Christ.

1. The Steps do not set us free. Christ sets us free in response to our faith, repentance, and submission to Him (John 8:36).

2. Believers begin to experience their freedom when they have an encounter with the truth, and Jesus is the Truth (John 8:32).

3. Christians must take responsibility for their own sins and cooperate with the Holy Spirit in order to experience their freedom.

4. Every liberated disciple of Jesus Christ can help others.

5. Christ is the Deliverer. We are not.

6. Sanctification is a process that requires our full participation.

Therefore, my dear friends, as you have always obeyed—not only in my presence, but now much more in my absence—continue to work out your salvation with fear and trembling, for it is God who works in you to will and to act according to his good purpose (Philippians 2:12-13).

Freedom in Christ for Leaders

As our church began to equip believers by leading them through the Steps, I became aware of my own need for complete repentance. One of the strongholds in my life was resentment toward my father due to years of physical and emotional abuse during my childhood. I was not aware of the depth of pain and resentment I had against him until the Holy Spirit brought it to light and I was able to forgive my father. The Lord graciously healed our relationship, and I experienced new growth in my relationship with God.

We encouraged all of our leaders to deal with strongholds by practicing the Steps on a regular basis. We minister freedom to others most effectively when we are free ourselves. We learned that freedom in Christ is not an event, but a lifestyle. We are constantly at war with the forces of darkness, and the only way to maintain our freedom is to live in submission to the Lord and to resist the enemy of our souls.

When leaders experience their freedom in Christ, they are able to serve much more effectively, and their ministries become more balanced and fruitful. We also learned about setting our church free.[1] Our leaders took yearly weekend retreats to process the Steps to Setting Your Ministry Free. The results were always extraordinary. We saw more joy, unity, and peace in our church, and we also usually grew numerically.

Key Needs Among Latinos

As I observe the current state of the Latino church, several spiritual needs stand out:

1. We need to experience God's grace and love in our families and churches in order to overcome the legalistic tendencies of our religious background.

2. We need to understand God's sovereign love and our identity in Christ to overcome a sense of fatalism and rejection that plagues our people. Most Latinos struggle with a negative self-image.

3. We need to proclaim God's truth and the authority of the Scriptures in order to overcome the many lies and superstitions of our culture.

4. We need to forgive, especially those of us who come from dysfunctional and broken families.

5. We need freedom from sexual strongholds. Adultery and fornication are ripping the very fabric of the Latino family.

6. We need to be free from fear. Drug lords and cartels have terrorized and paralyzed many of our communities.

7. We need to overcome addictions to drugs and alcohol.

8. We need to discover God's love and provision so we can be free from a mind-set of despair and poverty.

9. We need to learn to take personal responsibility for our lives.

10. We need to discover God as a loving Father who longs for an intimate relationship with His children. This will help us overcome a mind-set dominated by machismo.

11. We need to adopt the lifestyle of a true disciple so all believers are personally connected to Jesus Christ as their only source of life.

12. We need spiritual accountability in local churches.

13. We need to look to Jesus Christ as our only mediator in our relationship with the Father. No one else can take this place of prominence in our lives.

Freedom in Christ and the Great Commission

Jesus came to them and said, "All authority in heaven and on earth has been given to me. Therefore go and make disciples of all nations, baptizing them in the name of the Father and of the Son and of the Holy Spirit, and teaching them to obey everything I have commanded you. And surely I am with you always, to the very end of the age" (Matthew 28:18-20 NIV).

I have enjoyed watching the power of multiplication in the church. The message of freedom in Christ has led us to reproduce disciples and not simply make converts. We have learned to focus our ministry on faithful people who will in turn make other disciples. Just recently my wife and I were invited to a special dinner where six bivocational pastors thanked us for sharing Christ with them many years ago. Now they are planting churches and winning others for Christ. We praise our Lord and God, who is able to bring about multiplication in His kingdom.

I have learned over the years that mature, healthy believers are most effective in transmitting the life of Christ to others. Liberated disciples will multiply! The only way to get healthy is to pursue God with all of our hearts and to deal effectively with the spiritual and mental strongholds that inhibit our growth in Christ. This requires diligence and a firm stance in our faith. "For our struggle is not against flesh and blood, but against the rulers, against the powers, against the world forces of this darkness, against spiritual forces of wickedness in the heavenly places" (Ephesians 6:12). "The heavenly places" refers to the spiritual realm that seeks to enslave this world. We must keep in mind "that the whole world lies in the power of the evil one" (1 John 5:19). But we also must keep in mind (and help our people to believe) that He who is in us is greater than he who is in the world (1 John 4:4) and that Satan cannot touch us as long as we abide in Christ.

Freedom in Christ in Cuba

I had an extraordinary opportunity to serve the body of Christ on the beautiful island of Cuba. As the Lord opened the doors for ministry there, we introduced the pastors of an indigenous denomination to the Steps to Freedom in Christ. For several hours we taught and practiced the Steps in a group setting. When we got to the step of forgiveness, the pastors mentioned a splinter group that had left the denomination with 12 churches and their buildings. With tears in their eyes, the pastors forgave the group, and the Lord healed the pain caused by the division. The Spirit of joy permeated our gathering, and as they closed the meeting, they collected a love offering for the splinter group!

The Holy Spirit's work that day was remarkable because it brought healing to pastors who had bitterness against each other. After this day of genuine repentance, the denomination began to experience incredible growth. Every year the churches grew both spiritually and numerically. They were able to have a greater impact on unbelievers because they had dealt with their sin of division. Unity among believers is at the very core of Jesus' heart.

> My prayer is not for them alone. I pray also for those who will believe in me through their message, that all of them may be one, Father, just as you are in me and I am in you. May they also be in

us so that the world may believe that you have sent me. I have given them the glory that you gave me, that they may be one as we are one (John 17:20-22 NIV).

Our unity in Christ has a direct impact on the unbelieving community. The world has a much greater opportunity to believe if you and I are one in Christ. The experience in Cuba taught me that when believers are set free, Christ's life flows much more freely through them into a needy world.

An apple tree does not have to worry about producing fruit. If it's a healthy tree, it will produce abundant fruit. Many believers are reading self-help books to improve their marriages, succeed in their finances, improve their health, and overcome obstacles but with few lasting results. Nothing can help the church more than dealing biblically with sin issues that plague us. Nothing can substitute for a life filled with the Holy Spirit. When we experience this, the joy of freedom in Christ will spread throughout our relationships and cause a ripple effect in our families and communities.

A Vision for Latinos in the United States and Latin America

Growing up in a highly dysfunctional family and experiencing the devastating impact of generational and personal sin was difficult for me, but that experience has given me a greater appreciation for Christ's complete work of salvation. I know who I am in Christ, I have experienced the liberating power of the gospel, and I am in the process of being sanctified—these things have filled my heart with hope. God's people, their marriages, and their ministries can be set free in Christ. I have hope for the Latino church because the complete gospel of Christ is the only joyful message that can truly liberate us from the bondage of sin. This is the message the church has the privilege to proclaim and the responsibility to demonstrate. This is what Jesus came to do and what the church is commissioned to continue doing.

> The Spirit of the Lord is on me, because he has anointed me to preach good news to the poor. He has sent me to proclaim freedom for the prisoners and recovery of sight for the blind, to release the oppressed, to proclaim the year of the Lord's favor (Luke 4:18-19 NIV).

Glen and Katy Arias

Glen and Katy Arias were born and raised in Bogota, Colombia. During their early years, revolutionaries there struggled against what they thought was a tyrannical government. Over the course of a few decades, the battle changed, and the revolutionaries became little more than outlaws living in the jungle. To support their cause, they turned to drugs and kidnapping. On several flights to Colombia I was warned by our government not to go and told that if I was kidnapped, our government would not pay the ransom. Many professionals fled the country for fear of being kidnapped. Pastor Dario Silva-Silva discovered that his name was on a list to be kidnapped, and his board advised him to remain in Miami and to come back only when it was safe.

While I was on a recent trip to Colombia, a student-led protest was planned for a midday rally against the revolutionaries. People packed the streets to proclaim that they didn't support the revolutionary cause. It was very effective. By the time of my most recent trip to Colombia, the political situation had changed dramatically. The highways were patrolled by the military, and driving from city to city was safe again. Pastor Dario is free again to travel from the United States to Colombia.

Glen and Katy grew up in this hostile transition. While living in Colombia, Glen practiced law, and Katy was a psychologist. Here is their story.

Living in Colombia, South America

We have been Christians for several years and have received some very good teaching. We first heard of Freedom in Christ Ministries through our church, Casa Sobre la Roca. We made an appointment to be led through the Steps to Freedom in Christ, which became like a compass to direct our walk with the Lord. We were able to identify specific beliefs and actions that we needed to resolve, and this led to genuine repentance.

We felt secure in our relationship with God, but we had to leave Colombia. Glen was working on a difficult legal case, and an attempt was made on our lives. Although this remains a vivid memory, we believe the Lord protected us. We fled to the United States for one purpose— to serve God for the rest of our days. We identify with Joshua, who said, "As for me and my house, we will serve the LORD" (Joshua 24:15).

We arrived in the United States with seven suitcases, a five-month-old baby, and an application for political asylum. We were totally separated from our family, our cultural roots, and our chosen professions. We believed that God had a plan in all of this and would use the scraps of our lives. He bottled up our tears, used all of the bad experiences for eternal good, cleared up the confusion, and gave us new direction and an eternal purpose.

It was not easy at first. We experienced difficult times and heard many discouraging words from others who had made a similar transition. Their voices grew louder: *This country is very hard. Without credit, you are nothing. Without English, you're done. You have to do what you have to do. You have to work very hard. There won't be time for the family. Forget your professions—here you are second-class citizens.*

We battled fear and felt paralyzed by their words. In a moment of light we thought: *This is not the plan of God. His blessing is not to bring sorrow. We may be in the same situation as others, but we don't have to respond as they do or buy into their negative message.* When we were attacked in Colombia, God had a reason for saving our lives and giving us a new start. He has a plan, and we are not going to accept anything less than what He has for us. We are going to ask Him for great things, beyond what we could imagine. We are going to trust Him. He invited us to sit at His table, so we are not going to occupy the place of the dogs and eat the scraps under the table.

Contrary to the warnings, we received rapid approval of our status under political asylum, confirming again that we were supposed to be in the United States. One morning, when our savings were down to $20, we received a call from an American lawyer who needed the services of a Colombian lawyer. (We had sent out many resumes seeking work.) The pay for this work would be $250 per hour. After receiving this call, we had tears in our eyes, and we remembered the words of our Lord, "Be still, and know that I am God" (Psalm 46:10).

Through this experience we learned that God reigns and that we need to trust Him. He is not deterred by what people say or limited by our natural abilities. God revealed the deception behind the discouraging words that we had heard and believed. By the grace of God we were able to renounce those lies, believe the truth of God's Word, and not allow ourselves to be governed by circumstances. We learned from *Victory over the Darkness* that God established our identity as His children. We don't get our identity from our profession, our social status, our academic achievement, our family name, or our country of origin. We really are His children, and He will never leave us or forsake us. He has begun a work in us, and He will complete it in spite of adverse circumstances.

Shortly thereafter, we were asked to join the staff of our church. God's purpose for our lives became more clear as we became counselors and teachers in a theological institute organized by the church. Everywhere we turned, we encountered Hispanic people who were in the same condition we were: politically free but not spiritually free.

Our Ministry Experience

Our church in Bogota was an oasis. We could learn there in the comfort of our home environment. The work in Miami was much different, and we had to do battle in order to maintain our freedom. We had to receive ministry and restoration from the Lord so we could become useful vessels in the hands of the Potter as we counseled others and helped them find their own freedom in Christ. Pastor Dario Silva-Silva gave us this explanation:

> Latin America is not Europe or the United States or even herself. She is still looking for her own identity, and she may well find that identity in the gospel if it is interpreted in its own context and not under parameters that are foreign to it. At the same time, Hispanics who have been uprooted from their countries confront strange, upsetting sociological difficulties, and the churches are not understanding their needs.

God has called us to disciple the people of God who are exiled, who speak our native language, which is Spanish. We know from experience that they suffer from mental strongholds and that their minds need to be renewed by the Word of God. The words of Ezekiel became very real to us:

> He said to me, "Son of man, go to the house of Israel and speak with My words to them. For you are not being sent to a people of unintelligible speech or difficult language...whose words you

cannot understand. But I have sent you to them who should listen to you...Son of man, take into your heart all My words which I will speak to you and listen closely. Go to the exiles, to the sons of your people, and speak to them and tell them, whether they listen or not" (3:4-5,10-11).

The people in the community where we counsel and teach are thirsting to know God and draw closer to Him, but they are carrying a lot of cultural baggage and the syncretism of Latin America. They struggle with fear and confusion, not knowing how to resolve their personal and spiritual conflicts even though most have been Christians for years. Hispanic people have a very complicated spiritual environment. It is full of tradition, religiosity, and permissiveness under the influence of witchcraft and New Age, which are accepted in all social classes. On the other hand, in many areas of Latin America, evangelicalism is synonymous with ignorance, poverty, and even heresy. Consequently, many people cannot develop and mature in their relationship with Jesus Christ.

Latin America is now experiencing a revival, but this presents a problem for evangelicals who want to minister in the fullness of the Spirit. Without a biblical foundation, they venture into the unknown, opening the doors to legalism and fanaticism. The list of occult practices in Latin America is enormous and deeply embedded in the culture. The connection between these practices and the kingdom of darkness is ignored because they have been practiced for years as local customs.

We also encounter the general practices of the macho Latino. He is often unfaithful and irresponsible and doesn't care for his wife. She tolerates his infidelity and physical abuse for the economic support he sometimes gives. Generation after generation of Hispanic families have lived with this reality. Even Christians repeat this cycle and live under the bitterness of divorce and abuse. Having lived in a macho environment as children, many Christians have flawed understandings of God. Instead of seeing God as a loving Father, they believe He is distant and disinterested.

The Hispanic culture also struggles with a deeply rooted tendency toward rebellion, which often leads to anarchy. We have not been taught to renounce our personal or social rebellion, but have accepted them for decades. We have struggled to live with the abuse of power and corruption of many government leaders. Without genuine repentance, Christians will repeat the cycles of violence and poverty that they brought with them from their own countries.

The Hispanic community has struggled under the erroneous concept that we have to heal before we can forgive. Of course, that will prevent both healing and forgiveness. Inner healing is the result of forgiveness, which is a decision of the will. God holds us responsible for our own restoration (2 Corinthians 13:11), and this spiritual principle has been a personal guide in my (Katy's) professional development as a psychologist. I have seen people make choices that led to healing and freedom. People who had been given terrible diagnoses were set free when they resolved their personal and spiritual conflicts.

Pride is a universal problem, but it occurs again and again in our ministry. Many Christians do not realize that class consciousness, elitism, and racism have invaded their lives. The cultural shock that we experienced when coming to the United States included the realization that we were now in a minority status. What we were proud of before did not count for anything here. To adjust, we had to adapt to the simple truth: *I cannot do this alone. I need to depend on God.*

As we have continued to grow in the Lord, we have become more aware of Satan's attacks and the battle for our minds. This has reinforced the need for us to remain in Him. The Bible verses in *Victory over the Darkness* that depict who we are in Christ constantly remind us of the fundamental importance of being children of Almighty God. God will give us His direction for our lives, but we must confide and rest in Him.

Before long, God surprised us again. God led us to establish a small immigration counseling service, and we were invited to join the staff of Freedom in Christ Ministries as the coordinators for the southeastern region of the United States. God has changed our lives, provided for our needs, helped us to manage our time, and equipped us to serve with Freedom in Christ Ministries. In our church we have used the tools and methodology we have learned. They have helped us establish and maintain our own freedom, and we now have the privilege to help others. Recently we received the following letter from a teenager:

> When I was in seventh grade, I began hearing a voice at midnight that scared me. The voice caused me to believe many lies and told

me that I was worth nothing. I started wanting to die, and I didn't want to hear anything from God. I became very moody, began rejecting everyone around me, and just wanted to close myself in my own room.

Now, after having processed the Steps to Freedom in Christ with Dr. Katy Arias, I have felt a great peace in my life and in my heart. The fear and the voices that I have heard many times since I was a young child have finally disappeared. I renounced all of the lies Satan had placed in my mind. I regained a thirst to seek God and to learn much more about Him. God, through the Steps, helped me to understand that I am His daughter, that I am beautiful, that He has great things for me in the future, and that all the things that happened with me were Satan's tactics to destroy me.

We believe the Hispanic community has biblical knowledge and ecclesiastical activism but suffers from the lack of real solutions to personal and spiritual conflicts. We pray that the pastors of local churches will be able to understand the needs of their congregations and be equipped to lead their people to freedom in Christ through genuine repentance and faith in God. We are committed to use the message and method of Freedom in Christ Ministries to help them reach that goal.

9

Ministering Freedom to the African-American Church

Several years ago, while living in California, I recall hearing that the average Spanish-speaking student in the California school system completed only ten and a half years of education. That is partly due to the problem of language. The average African-American student completed eleven and a half years of education, and the average Caucasian student completed twelve and a half years of education. Asian Americans averaged thirteen and a half years of education.

Several factors contribute to those differences, but one major factor is the influence of legal and illegal immigration. Most of the illegal immigrants from Latin America come from the bottom of their culture, but the opposite is true for Asian immigrants. The African-American community has struggled more with racial inequality and the lingering effects of slavery.

The Hispanic culture in the United States generally has stronger family ties than does the African-American community. One of the tragedies of slavery was the damage it did to family units. Fathers could be sold separately from their families, leading to a matriarchal family structure. That impact is still being felt in America. That is why I am thrilled to introduce to you my friend and golfing partner, Daryl Fitzgerald. His name sounds Irish, but Daryl is an African-American pastor, and this is his story.

My Roots

I grew up in a small town in Virginia, the youngest of five children. My only sister had a rough time with four boys in the house. Our family did not have a lot of money, so we were encouraged to get a good education, believing that would give us a chance to have a better life. When my brothers and I were very young, my parents encouraged us to excel in sports and earn a college scholarship. That was our best opportunity to get the education we needed to fulfill the dream of living a quality life. I was not a big kid, but I was an above average athlete and played everything from soccer to basketball.

Sports came easy for me when I was young. I was a natural athlete and enjoyed the games. My stepfather (whom I will refer to as my father) worked hard to provide financial support, but he provided little emotional support. He loves sports to this day, but showing love and affirmation was very awkward for him. I tried to win his approval and earn his love and acceptance by being a good athlete. That was the only way I could connect with him and receive some positive emotional feedback. I poured myself into sports because I thought my father would be proud of me. I reasoned that if I played well, I would finally hear my father say, "I am proud of you," or "You did a good job." But instead, most of the time he said, "You could have done better!" When I did not play well, he yelled at me and called me terrible names, and I felt like a failure.

I learned from my father that I had to work for love and acceptance. Failing at sports was unacceptable, and making a mistake was not an option, because I thought that if I did not play well, I would lose his love and respect. Therefore I tried to win my father's approval by being the best basketball player I could be. Still, I never seemed to do well enough to feel appreciated. Of course, this would impact any boy's relationship with his heavenly Father. It was especially difficult for me because my earthly father was a pastor.

Early American Spirituals

Historically, in the black community, the church was the lifeline. It was the institution where African-Americans found encouragement and mutual support. The church provided a source of hope for those who tried to survive during the days of slavery. It was the only place where those in the African community could freely express themselves.

The church was the hub of the culture. It provided a safe environment where people were loved and accepted. They could talk about political and social issues without the fear of retribution. One of the ways the church community expressed itself was through singing spirituals. These were songs that oppressed and abused African-American slaves sang to hold on to the hope of finding a better life. The physical hardships and mental abuse many slaves suffered was brutal. Some of the songs portrayed a somber mood and were grievous and burdensome because they were reflections of the people's lives.

Although these songs were spiritual and talked about heaven, some served a dual purpose. These were encoded with secret messages about an escape route for slaves who wanted to flee from the hardship and abuse of slavery. Whenever slaves organized a time to escape from their slave masters, they sang these encoded songs to communicate important information to one another without being detected.

"Swing Low, Sweet Chariot" includes these lines: "I looked over Jordan and what did I see / Coming for to carry me home / A band of angels coming after me / Coming for to carry me home." A "home" was a place where all slaves could live free—heaven, yes, but also a free land, a place of safety for slaves to escape the bondage of slavery. "The Gospel Train" also includes coded messages: "The gospel train is coming...Get on board...For there's room for many a more." These phrases were direct calls for slaves to be prepared when the time came to run away and join others escaping from slavery. Such songs referred to the underground railroad, led by an antislavery community of men and women in Ripley, Ohio, who welcomed fugitive slaves.

Such songs were catalysts that led thousands of slaves to "the promised land"—that is, a land where they could be free. How wonderful these beaten-down people must have felt when they were finally free. Spirituals helped many find their freedom from slavery and are part of the rich history of the African-American church. Over the years, the church became one of the primary institutions in the African-American community that helped people overcome social injustices and achieve educational, social, and political freedom.

As an African-American growing up in the church in the 1970s, I was taught that if I wanted to obtain an education, church attendance was just as important as playing sports. Being at church every time the doors were opened was just as important as learning how to dribble a basketball or hit a baseball. I was not a rebellious kid, so I didn't have a problem attending church, but it didn't mean the same thing to me that it meant to the generations before me. It was not as important to me as it was for those who grew up in the days of slavery and segregation.

As a child, I never fully understood the rich heritage of our church or why we continued to sing some of the spirituals. Now, as an adult, I understand that these songs help many African-Americans remember how God has delivered us from slavery in the United States. We sing them for the same reason that Jews observe the Passover to celebrate and remember their rich heritage and to remember how God delivered their ancestors from their own slavery.

After the civil rights laws were implemented in America, visible changes began taking place in our society. However, changes in the African-American church community were not as forthcoming. We celebrated the victories of the civil rights movement, but we continued nursing our wounds and trying to overcome the emotional scars of slavery. Some churches did not see the need to change traditions, especially when it came to music, because some traditional songs continued to help many people endure rough times.

Singing those traditional songs never made a lot of sense to me because I did not understand the history behind them. As a child, I was not directly influenced by the spirituals, so they weren't appealing to me. I would think to myself, *I don't like singing these songs because they feel so sad*. I would see older men and women raising their hands and clapping, screaming and shouting, and jumping and running around the church. All the while I wondered, *What am I missing? What are they shouting about?* I remember church services lasting all day long. My overall church experience was as sad as the mournful songs!

Church and Basketball

Eventually, the glamour of sports eclipsed my involvement in the church. I continued to attend, but the services bored me. Church seemed to have a lot of rules. The more I attended, the more I heard the do's and don'ts of how I needed to live as a kid. I began mentally drifting away from church because it was just like home—I felt as if I had to perform in order to be accepted.

Church leaders constantly preached that loving the world and listening to secular music were sins, so I left our services feeling bad because I enjoyed listening to secular music. Even playing basketball was considered worldly because it could lead the wrong direction in life! I was discouraged by hearing all the things I could not do, so I became less attracted to church and more attracted to sports. In church services, I ended up feeling bad about myself. But on the field or on the court, people affirmed me for doing well.

I was getting pretty good at playing basketball, and it was slowly becoming an idol in my life. I began buying into my parents' idea that I could get a college scholarship and an education. I didn't totally abandon the church because I had attended enough services to know that one day I would need to have it as a part of my life. However, church attendance was just a religious activity. Basketball worked its way into my DNA because I saw that I was easily accepted for what I did as an athlete. At church I didn't hear that applause or feel that significance.

The preacher's sermons were not encouraging and were usually about either holiness or hell—holiness as the way to live and hell if you did not live it. Listening to some of these sermons was like being thrown in a boxing ring and getting hit with a one-two punch. Fear was the initial blow. After hearing the preacher yelling and shouting at the top of his voice over and over again, "You don't want to go to hell!" I totally agreed with him. I did not want to go to hell! But his sermons made me fearful that I would.

Holiness was the knockout punch. I felt the whack every time I failed to live up to the standard and rules of the church. When the preacher told stories of the men and women who lived in what he called "the Bible days" (Moses, Joseph, David, Esther, Mary, and so on) they all seemed to be perfect, which in my mind qualified them as saints. I thought God used those people to do great works because they learned how to live the way they were supposed to. I thought a saint was a person who learned how to become perfect. I heard over and over again that we should all be holy because God is holy (1 Peter 1:13), but I knew I was unable to live up to that standard. I tried my best to live the Christian lifestyle.

I gave my heart to Jesus nearly every Sunday because I was afraid of going to hell. I tried to live right, but it seemed that I was reminded each Sunday that I could do a better job. Church became a place of pain for me. It was a community aligned against the world and a place that reminded me where I was going when I died. Because I was unable to live the holy life, I was afraid to attend church and afraid not to.

I felt trapped and paralyzed at the same time. I was mentally tormented because I didn't know what was going to happen to me. As a child, I was often afraid to go to sleep because I thought if I died in my sleep, I would wake up in hell. The fear of dying and going to hell dominated my mind, especially during the night. I would lay in my bed and cry, trying not to go to sleep because I did not want to die. I was always happy to see the sun come up the next morning because that meant I made it through another night.

Spiritual Attack at Three in the Morning

Another church in our community promoted a special Friday night service featuring a must-see video on hell. It was highly publicized and created a lot of buzz. Kids were wondering what the video would be like, and some asked if I was going to attend. Reluctantly I agreed to go, but part of me did not want to go. I didn't want to give the impression that I was afraid, nor did I relish the thought of being called a punk. So I went.

The video was filled with scenes that described what happens to people in hell. After seeing how powerful Satan was portrayed in the video, I was terrified. This led to an unhealthy fear of Satan. Now I was not only afraid to go to church and afraid of dying but also afraid of the devil, his demons, and what they could do to me in hell. I began looking over my shoulder, fearing that the devil was coming after me, especially at night.

I began leaving my radio on all night to distract my mind from the fear of death and other tormenting thoughts. One night I was awakened around three in the morning. An eerie song was playing on the radio. As my eyes were adjusting to the darkness of the room, out of the corner of my eye I thought I saw something moving in the middle of the floor. I looked and saw a dark black silhouette of a man walking toward my bed.

I thought it was my brother playing around. I rubbed my eyes, hoping that it was just my imagination. When I opened them again, it was still in the middle of my bedroom. The weird music in the background was not helping matters! I closed my eyes, not wanting to believe what I was seeing, but even with my eyes tightly shut I could still see everything in my bedroom. That's when I freaked out. My mind was racing, and my heart sank with fear. I knew this thing in my room had come to take me to hell. I wanted to run out of my room, but I was afraid to move. The dark figure started walking toward my bed, got about a foot away from me, and disappeared.

Needless to say, I did not go back to sleep that night. For the rest of the night I thought about going to church to learn how to deal with the spiritual side of life. Fear became the major reason why I attended church, not God's love for me! If going to church could somehow help me get closer to God and keep the devil away from me, I was willing to go. I never told anybody what happened, and I sensed that no one wanted to talk about spiritual conflicts.

Spiritual Warfare

If you ask people in an African-American church if Satan is real, they will likely answer yes. However, most will also say or imply, "Don't mess with him." Such avoidance unintentionally elevates the fear of Satan and undermines our freedom. It gives Satan more control over religious people than over people who do not attend church. The fear of Satan is a major issue among African-American churches, and the subject is seldom discussed. Although I was taught to go to church every Sunday morning, afternoon, and evening and also on Wednesday evenings (for which I am truly thankful), I did not have adequate answers for all of the spiritual warfare I encountered as a child.

The media and many of our churches give the impression that Satan has more power than God does. Many people talk about fearing Satan more than they talk about fearing God. The Bible never says we should fear Satan, but it does teach that the fear of God is the beginning of wisdom. When we fear Satan more than God, we elevate him as a greater object of worship.

I remember hearing in church that Jesus has all power over the enemy, but the conversations in the church about demons or Satan were based on fear. I remember singing that Jesus is the answer for the world today, but I could not find any answers for my situation and the spiritual warfare I encountered. Consider the irony: As we saw earlier, the African-American church provided hope during the days of slavery, but my church was not addressing spiritual slavery. Clearly, my ancestors and I had very different experiences at church.

I was a spiritual slave to Satan, vulnerable to his schemes and unable to find my freedom. In my heart I somehow knew that Jesus was the answer for my problems, but I didn't know how He could help me. Though I was in church and sang about Jesus every Sunday, I never understood who He was and what He did for me. I never realized the power of the gospel, the essence of being a Christian, and the significance of being a child of God.

I remember seeing a picture of a white guy with a beard looking up to heaven (it was supposed to be a representation of Jesus), but I never understood the significance and meaning behind the picture. As a child, I never found adequate answers from the church concerning the problems I encountered. With so many unanswered questions about the spiritual world, it was only by the grace of God that I made it through that time in my life.

Sexual Sins

As a teenager growing up in the church, I noticed a tolerance for sexual sins. Talking about sexual issues in the African-American church was taboo. Sex was the main topic of discussion outside of the church, so I never understood why it was off-limits in the church. Conversations about sex and dating in the church were limited to two rules: Don't date, and don't have sex until you are married.

However, sexual sins were prevalent throughout the church. Homosexual behavior was and still is tolerated in the choir and throughout the community. It was too shameful to talk about. It was never openly addressed. Some Baptist preachers were known to have secret illicit relationships with women, but no one said anything or did anything to stop or confront the issues. Many African-Americans would say, "What goes on in the house, stays in the house." That type of attitude seemed to be in the church as well. What went on in the church sexually stayed in the church, and that left many men and women in bondage to sexual sins.

Liberty University

After many years of playing school sports, I received a scholarship to play basketball at Liberty University. When I signed my letter of intent to attend Liberty, the fact that it was a Christian school didn't matter—I was simply pursuing a good education. But there I heard a clear presentation of the gospel for the very first time. I heard that I did not have to die in my sin and go to hell, and that alone was good enough for me! I learned that Jesus Himself died on the cross to break the power of sin, to show me how much He loved me, and to offer me the gift of eternal life. In return, I simply had to put my trust in Him. That was good news to me, and I gladly gave my heart to the Lord!

Even though I gave my heart to Christ, I still had some challenges overcoming the fear of death and the spiritual influences I was introduced to as a child. Still, I began growing in my relationship with Him. He started becoming more important to me than playing basketball. Eventually He won first place in my heart, and I chose to give up my scholarship in order to pursue ministry.

Although my time on the basketball court was short lived at Liberty University, I didn't mind because I found peace with Jesus. I called my parents to tell them I was giving my basketball scholarship back in order to follow God and pursue ministry. The first thing they asked was where I was going to get the money to pay for school. That was a fair question, and I had no answer. I didn't know how I was going to pay for my education, but I was just as committed to God as I had been committed to getting a scholarship to play basketball. Giving up the very thing that I worked so hard for seemed crazy to my father, but that didn't matter to me. I felt as if a two-ton weight dropped off of my shoulders when I gave my scholarship back to the university. At last I didn't have to work to feel loved. I didn't have to be perfect and perform well in order to feel as if I was somebody. Doing God's work became my passion, and I wanted other teenagers to experience God as I had, especially in the African-American community.

I started meeting with two good friends at Liberty—Andre Sims and Chris Williamson—so we could hold each other accountable. One thing led to another, and we eventually started Transformation Crusade, an inner-city ministry designed to reach others for Christ using the language of the streets—hip-hop. The chancellor of Liberty University, Jerry Falwell, heard what we were doing and wanted to meet with us.

Dr. Falwell confessed to us that he did some things in the African-American community that he was ashamed of and wanted to make things right. We were blessed to share the moment with this man who was repenting before us. He realized that he may never be trusted again in the African-American community, but he wanted to support us in reaching our people in any way possible. He told us he heard from other pastors across the country of what we were doing as a ministry, and he wanted to help. Then he offered us full scholarships—even for masters' degrees if we chose to pursue that. My basketball career may have been short lived, but God gave "exceedingly abundantly above all that we ask or think" (Ephesians 3:20 NKJV). I finished college debt free and received the education my parents wanted for me, all without having to play basketball.

My Friend Neil

The unresolved issues from my past continued to loom over my head like a dark cloud. I still had not overcome the spiritual trauma I experienced as a child. After I graduated and moved to Nashville in the early '90s, I was invited to attend a Resolving Personal and Spiritual Conflicts conference. I had never heard of Neil, but the conference sounded interesting. My wife and I attended and heard answers to my questions about the spiritual attacks I experienced during my childhood. Neil asked a stunning question: "Has anyone ever been abruptly awakened at three in the morning?" Then he proceeded to explain what was going on spiritually at that time.

I wanted to know more, so I decided to purchase *Victory over the Darkness*. I had been searching for answers so long, I could hardly believe what I was reading. I began to understand and experience a level of freedom in Christ that I never understood before. I had not previously understood who I was in Christ and what it meant to be a child of God. I don't have to fear being alone, nor do I have to be afraid of the enemy, because God is with me. I am His child, and He is there to protect me. When I understood this, I began appropriating the truth that He will never leave me or forsake me (Deuteronomy 31:6).

Although I had been a Christian for many years, I began to feel confident in God's power and love for me, His child. I didn't feel as if God was judging, which is what I always felt as a child. I no longer felt rejected for not being perfect. I was learning to live under the new covenant of grace. I began understanding the magnitude and sacrifice of what Jesus did for me. He changed me from the inside out—from a sinner to a saint who sometimes sins. I cried and rejoiced for days as I began to understand God's love for me. The truth was setting me free (John 8:32).

One day, I purchased several of Neil's books at a local Christian bookstore, and the lady behind the checkout counter asked if I would like to meet Neil. I had no idea that he was living in the area. The following day I received a phone call from him, and we scheduled a lunch meeting. He agreed to do a Discipleship Counseling conference at our culturally diverse church. I expressed to Neil that I would love for people in the African-American community to understand and experience the reality of who they are in Christ, and I wanted to learn everything I needed to learn in order to help others find their freedom.

A lady from our congregation asked Neil for a personal appointment, and he asked me to sit in as a prayer partner. I was there to learn. Until that time I was reluctant to take the next step because of my own fears. What I experienced and saw God do in that appointment was amazing. No words can adequately summarize my feelings when I see what God does in these appointments. I can only say that God is real!

After watching Neil take someone through the Steps to Freedom in Christ, I knew I needed a personal appointment myself. The result was a spiritual cleansing for my soul. The issues from my childhood are resolved. The fear of death no longer has a hold on me, and I can honestly say that I am healthier spiritually, mentally, and emotionally. I am now a ministry associate with Freedom in Christ ministries nationwide, and I have personally led more than 50 people through the Steps.

Neil and I walk together as brothers. We are alive and free in Christ and partners in the gospel ministry. He is white and I am black...and that doesn't matter at all. Freedom in Christ has truly destroyed barriers of race and class. To this day Neil and I are good friends who play golf together whenever we can.

My Vision

My vision is to see others in the African-American community set free from the bondages of satanic lies and sexual sins. I pray that all Christians would come to know the truth about who they are as children of God and understand the freedom that Christ has purchased for them on the cross. We do not have to live in guilt and shame. We do not have to believe the lies of this fallen world. Satan is defeated. The key to our victory is to be alive and free in Christ. The battle has been won; we just need to proclaim the truth and help as many as we can be fully reconciled to God.

Rebuttal

As a child I sang in church, "Red and Yellow, Black and White. All are all precious in His sight." But it was merely a nice sentimental thought because I never saw another person who wasn't white until I was 14 years old. Racism entailed playful bantering between the Norwegians and the Swedes. Now I better understand the horrible sins of racism, sexism, and elitism. Rejecting others because they were born somewhere else is an insult to God. He is the one who created them.

We are in desperate need of "a renewal in which there is no distinction between Greek and Jew, circumcised and uncircumcised, barbarian, Scythian, slave and freeman, but Christ is all and in all" (Colossians 3:11). In other words, those of us who are alive in Christ are to have no racial, religious, cultural, or social distinctions. The gospel even transcends gender distinctions according to the apostle Paul (Galatians 3:28). The only way we can eradicate those barriers and unify the church is to help Christians become alive and free in Christ.

Every ethnic group currently needs people who can minister to their own. That will likely be true until all of us realize that we are one in Christ. Our growth process includes shifting our core identity away from our natural heritage and onto our spiritual heritage. Growing Christians are all moving in the same general direction—toward Christ—and the closer we get, the more unified we become. Allowing racial, social, and cultural barriers to separate us only reveals our immaturity.

Daryl's story brings up another issue that is critically important. All over the world, people are paralyzed by fear. Anxiety disorders include fear, anxiety, and panic attacks. Together they represent the number one mental health problem in the world, followed by depression. The world is experiencing a "blues" epidemic in an age of anxiety. (See the appendix for more information on overcoming fear and anxiety.)

Would you like to have my friend, colleague, and brother Daryl Fitzgerald come to your community and teach you how to resolve personal and spiritual conflicts? He would be happy to do so, and you can contact him through our U.S. office.

10

COMMUNITY
FREEDOM MINISTRIES

RICH MILLER

U.S. PRESIDENT, FREEDOM IN CHRIST MINISTRIES

Applause broke out after each silent testimony was displayed. It wasn't the polite, dutiful applause you get at events when spectators feel obligated to honor people they don't know. It was the applause of friends, cheering at victory statements that proclaimed the power of God to set captives free. Even youth and children were joining in joyful celebration with tears of gratitude.

The occasion was our church's thirteenth birthday party. Our community had officially become a teenager, and we were doing it up right. As the worship band played an instrumental background, several dozen men and women walked onto the stage. They carried cardboard signs that broadcast their bondage, written in big letters. But then they turned the signs over, and the other side proclaimed their freedom, written large enough for all to see. The applause erupted when each cardboard sign was turned and a message of defeat was transformed to a declaration of victory. Here are a few of them:

"Rejected. Self-hatred. Fear." On the other side the sign read "Set free."

"Lost in religious hypocrisy" was replaced by "Found by faith in God."

"Life was all about me" changed to "Satan lied, Jesus died, killed my pride."

"Lost and wanted to die" became "Now I have life."

"Lost and broken, addicted husband" transformed into "Found life, sober husband."

"Angry, scared, exhausted wife" changed into "Let go, let God, new life, new wife!"

"Destroyed by alcohol" radically transformed into "Rebuilt by God's grace."

"Fornicator, side-line Christian" replaced by "In the game, happily married."

The single word "Addict" changed into "Saved by grace; set free."

No one could miss the beauty of this transformation: "Sexual abuse, shame, rage" marvelously changed to "Precious daughter of the King."

The cheers are still resonating in my ears, and the vision of one triumphant brother pumping his fist into the air is still filling my mind's eye. It was a feast of joy and praise to God for saints rising out of the ash heap of broken lives. These were living, breathing trophies of God's grace, each of whom were silently proclaiming, "I run the path of your commands, for you have set my heart free" (Psalm 119:32 NIV).

Think of those 24 brave people at New Life Community Church in Asheville, North Carolina. They didn't hide their sin, and they boldly proclaimed their freedom. That procession of brokenness and restoration demonstrated God's desire for every church. It described what Jesus came to do and what He wants to do in your church and community.

More than 600 years before the birth of Jesus of Nazareth, the prophet Isaiah foretold the mission of the Messiah:

> The Spirit of the Lord GOD is upon me, because the LORD has anointed me to bring good news to the afflicted; He has sent me to bind up the brokenhearted, to proclaim liberty to captives and freedom to prisoners; to proclaim the favorable year of the LORD and the day of vengeance of our God; to comfort all who mourn, to grant those who mourn in Zion, giving

them a garland instead of ashes, the oil of gladness instead of mourning, the mantle of praise instead of a spirit of fainting, so they will be called oaks of righteousness, the planting of the LORD, that He may be glorified. Then they will rebuild the ancient ruins, they will raise up the former devastations; and they will repair the ruined cities, the desolations of many generations (Isaiah 61:1-4).

That is precisely what Jesus came to do, one life at a time, one church at a time, one community at a time. You can almost see the silent cardboard testimonies as the saints march triumphantly across the stage of heaven:

"Afflicted" turned around to read, "Brought good news."

"Brokenhearted" transformed to "Heart bound together and healed."

"Captive" changed to "Liberated!"

"Prisoner" became "Set free."

"Mourning" turned to "Comforted."

"Spirit of fainting and heaviness" to "Mantle of praise."

Imagine millions of saints from every tribe, tongue, people, and nation testifying to the grace of God and of their freedom in Christ.

This powerful and hope-filled passage of Scripture (Isaiah 61:1-4) includes a seamless and compelling transition. The first two verses focus on the Messiah (notice the use of *me*); the last two verses shift their attention to those to whom the Messiah ministers. *They* will be called oaks of righteousness. *They* will be the planting of the Lord, that He may be glorified. *They* will rebuild. *They* will raise up. *They* will repair the ruined and desolated cities.

It is clear. Before the people of God can grow strong, stable, and mature, they must be set free. Before the people of God can have a transforming impact on the culture and community around them, they must be set free.

When we look at verses like Isaiah 61:1-4, our minds can turn to those we know who are deeply oppressed by the enemy, those who are swirling down into the black hole of depression, or those chained by sexual, chemical, or gambling addictions. Then we gaze toward heaven and think, *Yes, Lord, thank You for coming to set these captives free*. He has come to do that— willingly and powerfully.

But the message and ministry of freedom is not just for those on the ragged edge of the church. It is for the pastor, the elder, the deacon, the minister's wife, the Sunday school teacher, the missionary, the nursery worker...the average Joe or Josephine sitting in the hardwood pew or on cushioned, upholstered chairs. It is for the child and the senior citizen, the teen and the parent, those married and those single. It is for you and me. It is for all God's people because *freedom* is a crucial part of *discipleship*.

Let's be honest. If the majority of Christ's followers were truly walking by the Spirit in grace, liberty, and truth, an awakening would have broken out in our nation long ago. Even though the sins of the general congregation may not be as blatant as those of the addict, they are more pervasive and ultimately just as spiritually deadening. We see control issues stemming from pride, fear, and deep insecurity. We see greed and materialism that dull our thirst for God and drown life in staggering debt. We see stress and anxiety from overwork and need of rest, and marriages slowly disintegrating as lust grows hot and love grows cold. We see religious duty without passion for Christ, and grudges nursed and bitterness justified from wounds licked for years. The list is endless.

Have we missed the real thing? We have believed that if we get people saved, plug them into biblical curriculum, and wait, we'll see them become mature Christians. We wish it were that easy, but it's not. Many church leaders have not found the bridge between salvation and maturity. It is the reality of *freedom* that comes from genuine repentance and faith in God. What is needed is a biblical means for resolving personal and spiritual conflicts so we can be set free from our past and established alive and free in Christ. Consider Hebrews 12:1-2:

> Therefore, since we have so great a cloud of witnesses surrounding us, let us also lay aside every encumbrance and the sin which so easily entangles us, and let us run with endurance the race that is set before us, fixing our eyes on Jesus, the author and perfecter of faith.

Imagine a group of runners preparing for a marathon. They are stretching their muscles, eager for the starter's pistol to signal the beginning of the race. As you look more closely, you notice something very strange about most of the athletes. They are wearing heavy backpacks, and some sort of vine seems to be wrapped around their legs.

The gun goes off, and those who are free from those burdens and bondages take off swiftly and joyfully. You know the race will be hard for them, but you have confidence they will reach the finish line. The others who are weighed down and tangled up are stumbling, falling, getting up, taking a few more steps, collapsing again, crawling, and pounding the ground in frustration.

Those discouraged, defeated runners certainly *don't* need someone to yell at them and tell them to stop being such slackers and work harder. Rather, they need someone to show them how to throw off those burdensome backpacks and get rid of those entangling vines of sin. Some runners must be convinced they need to be set free. Some must come to the point of desperation before they ask for help. Ultimately, they are responsible to throw off the burdens and sins, but they probably never will if they don't know how. Those who do will join the race and finish strong.

Imagine a congregation where grace is operative and an increasing number of attendees are living it out. A church where the leaders are choosing to face their own issues of baggage and bondage with honesty and transparency and are themselves walking in freedom, encouraging others to join them in their journey. A church where spiritually discouraged and defeated runners have a safe place to go to resolve their personal and spiritual conflicts. A church that is not yet perfect in Christ by any means but is progressing in Christ by all means.

Wishful thinking? A naive, idealistic utopia that can't happen this side of heaven? I don't think so. Let me introduce you to some groups around the country that might give you hope and kindle your vision for your congregation.

Escondido, California

Jim Learned is the consummate pastor. He is wise, gentle, caring, humble, and capable. He is not perfect, of course, but a good friend, husband, father, and grandfather. He started the North County Freedom Ministry (NCFM) out of Emmanuel Faith Community Church (Escondido, California) on the heels of Neil's conference there in October 1995. That Community Freedom Ministry (CFM) is still going strong under the leadership of Sharon Chapman. Though Jim has retired, he still instructs and encourages CFM coordinators in the western part of the United States.

Jim shared, "My greatest joy as a pastor has come from witnessing the resurrection power of Jesus Christ accomplish His work as the power of bondage is broken in hundreds of lives."

"Hundreds" is not an exaggeration. Including Neil's initial conference ministry at the church and the subsequent inception of the NCFM, 1400 people have been directly touched by the teaching message of freedom, including 540 attending video conferences and 216 in attendance at Overcoming Depression seminars.

"Taking individuals through the Steps to Freedom in Christ has been the heart of the ministry," Jim added. The NCFM has faithfully taken more than 400 inquirers (those seeking help) through the Steps in one-on-one appointments led by 45 trained and certified encouragers (lay counselors).

One of the most arresting things about the NCFM is that a prayer meeting on behalf of their ministry has been held *every week without exception* since its birth. Jim and the current director, Sharon, give all the credit to God for the fruitfulness and sustainability of this CFM in response to prayer. This ministry has truly lived, breathed, and moved forward on its knees.

Another important factor in the life of the NCFM is that it has always functioned under the authority of the leadership of Emmanuel Faith Community Church. Jim commented on this critical issue:

> When this ministry began, our senior pastor enthusiastically endorsed the biblical principles of our identity as children of God in Christ, the power of Christ's forgiveness for freedom and in relationships, and the work of God the Holy Spirit in the life of the believer. As the care pastor, I have had the joy of serving the pastoral staff and congregation with this core message.

The beauty of this CFM is that it has reached beyond the four walls of Emmanuel Faith Community Church, reaching out with a recovery ministry called Set Free, Christ-Centered Recovery and helping other congregations in southern California establish CFMs.

Jim concluded by saying, "We have been a part of kingdom building among other churches as together we have witnessed the fulfillment of Isaiah 61:1-4. Christ is fulfilling His promise to bind up the brokenhearted, give liberty to captives, and bring good news to the afflicted."

NCFM has hosted regional Catalyst events sponsored by Freedom in

Christ Ministries (FICM), where representatives from churches around Southern California and beyond have come to learn how to start and grow a CFM in their community.

Salem, Oregon

The Pacific Northwest is notorious for being the most unchurched region of the United States. However, where sin abounds, grace superabounds (Romans 5:20). FICM ministry associates (certified volunteers) Keith Swanson (a professional counselor) and his wife, Lindy, oversee a CFM in Salem, Oregon. Operating through Capital Park Wesleyan Church and Oasis (a Nazarene Church), the Swansons are seeing the Lord Jesus impact a growing network of lives in that part of the country. Here is Keith's report:

> Capital Park Wesleyan Church is an inspiration and support for the growth of CFMs in Oregon. Leaders from the freedom team have trained people from seven other churches to be encouragers and teachers of the FICM message. They continue to provide support to these individuals as they take the message and ministry back to their churches. God is now raising up interest in CFMs in other Wesleyan churches. Two pastors who have already started using FICM resources have expressed a desire for assistance in the development of freedom ministries at their churches.

Lindy shared what she is doing in her church.

> I am coleading the *Freedom in Christ Small Group Bible Study* DVD series and also taking people through the Steps to Freedom in Christ. I have seen people's countenances change from glum and angry to smiling and peaceful. I have seen people's characters change from depressed, bitter, defeated, withdrawn, and tormented to joyful, hopeful, peaceful, loving, and accepting. Instead of hiding from and repelling others, they are drawing others into fellowship through their love and care. They have gone from being needy to being partakers and givers in the life and fellowship of the church.

Community Freedom Ministries are about God's people coming out of darkness into light and being transformed from victims into victors in Christ. They are now able to serve the people in their church and community in the joy of their newfound freedom. A woman that Keith and Lindy ministered to through their CFM shared her story:

> I decided to take the Freedom in Christ class because it sounded good. I enjoyed the videos and the interaction with others, but as the class progressed, I started feeling more uncomfortable because I was hurt deep in my soul. Every time I saw a particular person, I felt physically sick. I went to great lengths to avoid this person because of a deep betrayal of trust and the fear of being hurt again. I had a shell of protection around me, or so I thought. That shell actually kept me from reaching out for help and kept me from being all I could be.
>
> I had gone through a process similar to the Steps before and I thought, *Okay, I've been there, done that, and bought the T-shirt.* (I actually have a sweatshirt that says Free at Last). But this time was different. I was desperate and tired of living like this, and things were getting worse inside me. When I finished the Steps, I thought, *Okay, that's done,* not really expecting too much. But I knew I had really meant what I did in repentance and forgiveness from my heart. As the days followed, I could feel a growing excitement inside of me. But the real test came a few days later.
>
> I was attending an event when I came face-to-face with the person who had hurt me so deeply. I started to do what I usually did—assess the situation and look for a place to run. Instead, my body had a mind of its own, and I walked right up to the person and shook hands. *Wait a minute! Why did I do that?* No one was more shocked than me. But it felt good. Later, as the person started speaking to the group, I was amazed. I just sat there with no sick feeling, no running out of the room as I had done in the past. Tears were streaming down my face because I no longer felt any pain. Later that person came to me and wanted to give me a hug. I said sure.
>
> Now I can pray, read the Bible more clearly, and talk more

freely to anyone who might be in a position to hurt me. Free
at last! Thank God Almighty, I'm free at last!

This woman adds an epilogue to her story above, explaining why she
needed to go through the process of forgiving again even though she
thought the work was already done.

> As I thought about this, I asked God, *How can this be? I
> thought I had forgiven already. Why is there such a difference this
> time?* He gave me an example. When you clean windows, you
> spray, wash, dry, and wipe clean. Or so you think. Then when
> the sun shines through, you look at the window again and see
> the streaks and spots you left behind. So you have to wipe it
> some more to get it completely clean. Before the sun shined,
> you thought it was clean, but you couldn't see clearly enough.
> You couldn't see the problem was still there. But once the sun
> shined through the window, you could see the dirt that hadn't
> been completely removed.
>
> Since my freedom appointment, I am experiencing a true life
> of freedom. I am hearing God's voice again and gaining more
> and more freedom. I love it, and my prayer is to see more
> people experience this freedom. Now I'm teaching freedom
> classes and leading others through the Steps. I praise God for
> bringing me to freedom in Christ.

On September 22, 1862 President Abraham Lincoln made the Emancipation Proclamation, which took effect 100 days later on January 1, 1863.
That proclamation read in part, "All persons held as slaves within any State
or designated part of a State...shall be then, thenceforward, and forever free."

Though the utterance of that proclamation did not end the actual practice of slavery (it took a war with the shedding of blood to move toward
that end), Lincoln's words ignited the hearts of millions of Americans and
changed the course of the war. Subsequent to the enactment of the proclamation, every advance of federal troops expanded the rule and reign of
freedom.

As it turned out, those who were set free from slavery became freedom fighters themselves. The liberated became liberators. By the end of
the Civil War, nearly 200,000 black soldiers and sailors had fought for the
Union and for freedom.

The Lord Jesus has uttered His emancipation proclamation: "If you abide in My word, you are My disciples indeed. And you shall know the truth, and the truth shall make you free...Therefore if the Son makes you free, you shall be free indeed" (John 8:31-32,36 NKJV).

The experience of bondage and slavery has not ended, even in the church. Jesus' shed blood and victory over evil supernatural rulers has made freedom possible. Every time the Lord raises up leaders to start a ministry of freedom, every time a Community Freedom Ministry is birthed and grows to be fruitful, and every time someone goes through the Steps to Freedom in Christ with a humble, open heart, the rule and reign of freedom in America expands. We have seen it all over the nation and the world: The liberated are still becoming liberators!

Colorado Springs, Colorado

Maybe you feel inadequate to start something like this in your church. Let me introduce Ken and Jan Hardison. They know exactly how that feels because they started building a CFM at their church from the ground up.

Ken (a retired airline employee) and Jan (a former teacher), who hail from Colorado Springs, Colorado, first heard Neil speak at a conference in Cottonwood, Minnesota, several years ago. They got excited about the message and studied Neil's bestsellers *Victory over the Darkness* and *The Bondage Breaker*. They then received permission to teach these books at their church and saw lives changed. But the Hardisons weren't immediately sold on the idea of starting a CFM. They dipped their toes in the waters for several years before they finally plunged in. Jan explained some of their preliminary work.

> The first step in our plan was to familiarize the entire church leadership team with the content of the freedom message. We hosted groups of leaders at our home for dinner and explained what it was all about. Later we studied *Victory over the Darkness* together. They all agreed with the content as well as the distinct need for it at our church (Discovery Christian Church).

Greg Lindsey, pastor of Discovery Christian Church, added this:

> One of the greatest challenges I have faced both in my own walk with God and in the ministry of leading others to grow

in Christ is the nagging question that never seems to go away: Is this it? Despite all our great books, studies, curricula, and formulas, the accompanying life that we most often offer feels like anything but freedom. The broken places, wounds, hurts, and pains in our individual stories don't simply evaporate when we come to Christ. For some time here at Discovery we have sought to walk with people, helping them face their places of brokenness and wounding as they seek their desperate need for healing and restoration. The question has been, what do you do once you get to that place of need? We now have the answer. Our CFM will prepare us to help people in our church and our entire community. Finally we are getting equipped to help people find not only Jesus, but also the life that their heart is longing for—a life that is free.

After their initial caution, Ken and Jan are convinced of God's calling on their lives. They plan on using the *Freedom in Christ Small Group Bible Study* to launch their CFM there in Colorado Springs, with the desire to train many encouragers in their church in the days ahead.

Ken and Jan have already multiplied their efforts by ministering in Casper, Wyoming, where Leigh White is starting a CFM. As best we know, Leigh's pioneering work is creating one of the first CFM outposts of freedom in the Cowboy State.

Springfield, Missouri

From the mountains to the prairies. Chapo (a retired cowboy) and Peg McCabe are the kind of folks you'd like to have Thanksgiving dinner with. They are down-to-earth, hospitable, solid, caring, godly, and seasoned veterans of the faith. The McCabes reside in the Show Me State of Missouri. Since 1997 they have been overseeing Freedom in Christ of the Ozarks, and their simple, Spirit-led, prayer-saturated strategy is bearing much fruit in the city of Springfield and in surrounding communities.

Chapo and Peg have assembled a ministry team of 17 others who have experienced their own personal freedom and wish to pass it on. Members of the team have been freed from a variety of strongholds including homosexuality, fear, and abuse, and they have found the ministry "marvelously addictive."

In 1999, church leaders asked Chapo and Peg to teach a freedom class during Sunday school. Peg wrote a study notebook based on one of Neil's conferences and distributed the notebooks and teaching cassettes to participants. Students listened to the cassettes at home, answered the questions in the notebook, and were ready to discuss the material the next Sunday. The discussions were so intense and created such interest that the class was extended to two hours each week.

The class quadrupled in size, with two more evenings of group study added. After that, word spread throughout the area of what was going on until now there are at least twelve churches representing six different denominations involved with Freedom in Christ of the Ozarks.

Members of the ministry network are also taking the freedom message to men's and women's homeless shelters as well as jails. A youth program is being developed that can be utilized in all the churches. Peg commented on what God has been doing in Missouri.

> The impact of a CFM network is like ripples on the water. One life changed produces a desire to see others walk in the freedom of their inheritance in Christ. They then reach others, and the effect multiplies through the power and grace of the Holy Spirit.
>
> Networks move the message faster and more widespread than any one individual or couple could possibly do. A network keeps those who are ministering from being isolated and provides a close-knit, common-purpose group of children of God, reproducing as they go.
>
> One of our members sent us an e-mail just before taking someone through the Steps. "Today is our third wedding anniversary, and we couldn't be happier! We have struggled through some tough times, but God has been faithful and has not only brought us through but also made us stronger. None of this would have been possible without the Freedom in Christ ministry, and that is why I am so proud to be a part of it."

When the apostle Paul was writing his parting words to his spiritual son, Timothy, he gave an exhortation that serves as a strong motto or credo for Community Freedom Ministries.

> You therefore, my son, be strong in the grace that is in Christ Jesus. And the things that you have heard from me among many witnesses, commit these to faithful men who will be able to teach others also. You therefore must endure hardship as a good soldier of Jesus Christ. No one engaged in warfare entangles himself with the affairs of this life, that he may please him who enlisted him as a soldier. And also if anyone competes in athletics, he is not crowned unless he competes according to the rules. The hardworking farmer must be first to partake of the crops. Consider what I say, and may the Lord give you understanding in all things (2 Timothy 2:1-7 NKJV)

God is looking for those who have been revolutionized by His grace, who live under the new covenant of grace and treat others with grace. Only when you've been transformed by the grace of God can you minister fruitfully in grace. Yes, it is hard work, this is a war, and we need to abide by the standards of the Word of God. We have heard from North Carolina, California, Oregon, Colorado, Wyoming, Missouri, and we conclude that it is worth the fight. Even more importantly, this work is well pleasing to our Commanding Officer, the Lord Jesus Christ.

Manhattan, New York

Manhattan is our last stop on our whirlwind journey of freedom around the country. Kristen Somody-Whalen is a professional photographer whose work has appeared in *Vogue, Harper's Bazaar, People,* and *Reader's Digest* magazines. She has snapped shots of Tom Cruise, Katie Holmes, Beyonce Knowles, and many other celebrities. But her greatest passion is spreading the message of freedom. Here is some of her story.

> Having been raised in a Christian home, I was shocked to discover after living a defeated Christian lifestyle for 26 years that I was not a sinner, but a saint who sins! Why didn't anyone tell me that before? From as far back as I could remember, I had been stuck in that sin-confess-sin-confess cycle. After learning the truth about my new identity as a child of God, my new position in Christ, my security, and my acceptance in Christ, my intimate relationship with the Lord took off like a racehorse out of its gate.

Kristen and her husband, Seth, have led a Bible study for people in the fashion and entertainment industry. They have seen a *Fox News* political analyst, a *Reader's Digest* creative director, a Louis Vuitton runway model, a published poet, and many others go through the Steps to Freedom in Christ. However, a fruitful ministry does not guarantee a pain-free life. Late in 2009, as Seth and Kristen entered into a time of rest from ministry and considered bringing the message and ministry of FICM to their new church, they received some difficult news. Kristen shares what happened.

> In September of 2009, my husband and I were three months along in a pregnancy for our first baby. A routine three-month checkup revealed that we had lost it. I was devastated. By November I was completely convinced that I was unloved, unsafe, uncared for, and unprotected. I began living as if those lies were true. I lost my joy. I was tired all the time. I felt hopeless.
>
> That December I was invited to take part in a pilot test of CFM University with FICM. I was amazed! I had been waiting six years to do this! This was my vision, my passion! At the same time, I was in a dark place spiritually, angry at God and the world. I thought to myself, *But right now, I can't even tell people in a convincing way that God is good and that He can be trusted.*
>
> My husband and I talked and prayed about it, and I knew I was to step out in faith. So I said yes and read through *Victory over the Darkness* and *The Bondage Breaker* again. The Lord was using these books to counsel me back to freedom. I realized that because of my great loss, I had become vulnerable to the lies of the enemy at such a critical time in my ministry. I swiftly renounced the lies I had believed and announced the truth that I was loved, safe, cared for, and protected in Jesus.
>
> The change in me was literally instantaneous. My joy returned to overflowing. I had more energy, hope, and passion for the Lord and for the message of freedom than I had even before the miscarriage!
>
> As I attended CFM University, I felt empowered and equipped as I began to fully understand how a Community Freedom

Ministry worked. The Lord gave me a plan, a vision, and the practical knowledge I needed to move forward. Before I left Knoxville, I e-mailed my church pastors and let them know what I was up to. Our lead pastor replied to my e-mail and said, "Brilliant. I love it. Make it happen."

Kristen is now moving ahead with training eight leaders from her church. One pastor has already been set free from a lifelong bondage to claustrophobia. Another pastor is now reading *The Bondage Breaker.* People in their church and community are lining up for freedom appointments and saying, "Finally! We have been praying for a ministry like this to start in our church for years."

I don't believe Kristen's church is alone in this yearning. We are asking God to raise up a Community Freedom Ministry (CFM) for every 30,000 people in this nation. For a nation of over 300 million, that's 10,000 CFMs!

Maybe you're the person to start one of them. Maybe God is calling you to step out in faith and start a Community Freedom Ministry. A CFM is simply a "freedom presence" in a church or community. That freedom presence involves *presenting* the message of freedom using FICM resources, *leading* people through the Steps to Freedom in Christ, and *training* individuals to use the Steps in personal freedom appointments. It's pretty basic and simple, but it requires the calling of God and the grace of God to be effective.

You might be wondering how you can get trained. We have an online training process called CFM University that concludes with a four-day person-to-person practicum that will jump-start you in developing a CFM in your hometown. Go to our website, www.ficm.org, and register. We will equip you and walk with you as you get up and running. If God is calling you, don't wait. Take a step of faith like Kristen did and watch Him work on your behalf.

Kristen is starting a CFM in Manhattan and anticipates the Lord raising up hundreds of CFMs in New York City alone. She said, "The time is now! God is doing a new thing here in New York, and people are ready to learn the truth that sets them free!"

I agree. Our nation is in moral decay. If ever the time was right and ripe for the people of God to discover freedom, walk in freedom, and spread the good news of freedom in Christ, it is now. The night comes, when no one can work. Let us do the works of God while it is still day. Sunset may come faster than we know. But for now, let us walk in the light as God Himself is in the light, for the Sunrise from on high has visited us "to shine upon those who sit in darkness and the shadow of death, to guide our feet into the way of peace" (Luke 1:78-79). Won't you join us?

Starting a Discipleship Counseling Ministry in Your Church

Most Christians and seekers are coming to our churches with a lot of baggage, and we need to help them resolve their personal and spiritual conflicts through genuine repentance and faith in God so they can be established alive and free in Christ. But where do we start? That is the most common question church leaders ask us.

Freedom in Christ Ministries began with Neil's books and expanded into a conference ministry with the Living Free in Christ conference for the general public. During the day, leaders were trained to do Discipleship Counseling. The Living Free in Christ conference is now available as a curriculum for Sunday schools, small groups, and home Bible studies. The course is titled *Freedom in Christ Small Group Bible Study* (Gospel Light, 2008). The course includes a DVD with 30-minute messages for each lesson as well as a teachers' guide that has all the messages written out so that leaders can either present the message themselves or play the DVD. The course also has a *Learner's Guide*, which includes the Steps to Freedom in Christ. Each participant should have a copy of the *Learner's Guide*.

This course is the entry point for churches, but it is not the end. For some it will be a new beginning on their journey to freedom and wholeness. If participants have no additional issues to resolve, they can use the *Daily Discipler* to digest a practical theology in five days a week for a year. After the course, some people will need additional help for residual flesh patterns, such as sexual addiction, chemical addiction, anger, fear, anxiety, depression, and reconciliation with others. Freedom in Christ Ministries has resources for all those, as we will explain later.

The next step is to help marriage partners become one in Christ. The book for that is *Experiencing Christ Together* and includes Steps for Beginning Your Marriage Free and Steps for Setting Your Marriage Free. The book and the Steps for Beginning Your Marriage Free are intended for premarital counseling. *Experiencing Christ Together* and the Steps for Setting

Your Marriage Free are for Sunday school classes, small groups, and home studies. Modified Steps are available when only one partner participates.

These marriage steps follow the same reasoning as the individual Steps to Freedom. That is, Christ must be included in the process, which usually takes a full day to accomplish. We recommend that people read the book, discuss it with a group, and then attend a weekend retreat. This powerful process helps couples resolve their conflicts by the grace of God.

The final step is for the church board and ministerial staff to resolve the church's conflicts and set the church or ministry free. The book for that, *Extreme Church Makeover*, explains servant leadership and lays the foundation for corporate conflict resolution. The Steps to Setting Your Church Free is a process that the board and staff work through, and that usually requires a day and an evening to process.

People must establish their individual freedom before processing the marriage and church Steps. That is why they should engage the Freedom in Christ course before attempting to resolve marital or corporate conflicts. If your church is full of people in bondage to sex, alcohol, drugs, bitterness, gambling, legalism, and so on, and if the marriages in your church are suffering, you have a church in bondage.

Neil has written a book entitled *Restored*, which is an expansion upon and illustrates the Steps to Freedom in Christ. Christians can work through this book on their own and facilitate their own repentance. That is possible because God is the One who grants repentance, binds up the brokenhearted, and sets the captives free.

Discipleship Counseling Training

We estimate that 85 percent of the participants who attend the Freedom in Christ course can work through the Steps to Freedom on their own. The book *Restored* may bump that percentage even higher. For those who can't work through the process on their own, we offer comprehensive training through books, CDs, DVDs, and study guides.

The material for training encouragers includes books, study guides, and several series of CDs and DVDs. (Each series comes with a corresponding syllabus.) Trainees receive the most thorough training when they watch the videos, read the books, and complete the study guides. To train encouragers, plan on scheduling two hours per week for 16 weeks. The material should be presented in this order:

Basic Training

SESSIONS 1–4

Video/audio: *Victory over the Darkness*
Reading: *Victory over the Darkness* and *Victory over the Darkness Study Guide*

SESSIONS 5–8

Video/audio: *The Bondage Breaker*
Reading: *The Bondage Breaker* and *The Bondage Breaker Study Guide*

SESSIONS 9–16

Video/audio: *Discipleship Counseling* and *Helping Others Find Freedom in Christ*
Reading: *Discipleship Counseling* and *The Bondage Breaker— the Next Step*

Books for Advanced Training

Overcoming a Negative Self-Image
Overcoming Addictive Behavior
Overcoming Doubt
Overcoming Depression
Winning the Battle Within
Freedom from Fear
Christ-Centered Therapy (for professional counselors)
Getting Anger Under Control
The Path to Reconciliation
A Biblical Guide to Alternative Medicine
Breaking the Bondage of Legalism
Praying by the Power of the Spirit
The Core of Christianity

The book *Discipleship Counseling* has further instructions for how to set up a Discipleship Counseling ministry in your church. We don't want to add to the workload of the pastoral staff. In fact, Discipleship Counseling can greatly reduce their load and equip lay people to do the work of ministry. Contact us for more information.

Freedom in Christ Ministries
9051 Executive Park Drive Suite 503
Knoxville TN 37923

(865) 342-4000

info@ficm.org
www.ficm.org
www.ficminternational.org

OVERCOMING ANXIETY DISORDERS

Processing the Steps to Freedom in Christ resolves the bondage to many fears. Regardless of what the presenting problem is, we always start by leading inquirers through the Steps. The process exposes and eliminates the influence of Satan, but more importantly, it removes the barriers to their intimacy with God. This allows the Spirit of God to work through them in a liberating way, enhancing the growth process. Lingering fears may remain, but many are overcome as people mature.

Phobias are learned, irrational fears, and they are often the result of traumatic experiences. Needless to say, they have to be unlearned, and that often requires a process rather than an event.

Fear is a God-given emotion. Anytime our physical or psychological safety is threatened, fear is the natural response. Anxiety is like fear without a clear cause. We are anxious because we don't know what is going to happen.

Anxiety is also a God-given response and can indicate concern. If you had an important exam tomorrow, you would naturally sense a little anxiety. The proper response is to let your anxiety prompt you to prepare adequately for the exam. If your teenager didn't come home on time, you should be a little anxious. Your anxiety can remind you to pray and take action. Jesus gave us the anecdote to free-floating or long-lasting anxiety in the Sermon on the Mount, and all Christians need to learn how to cast their anxiety onto Christ, who cares for them.

Fear, on the other hand, has an object, and fears are categorized by the object. Claustrophobia is a fear of enclosed places, agoraphobia literally means a fear of the marketplace, arachnophobia is a fear of spiders, and so on. The fear of God, however, is the beginning of wisdom, and that is the one fear that can expel all other fears. God is the only legitimate fear object. Fear of any other object is mutually exclusive to faith in God.

Two worksheets are included below. The first is entitled Overcoming Anxiety. The second is entitled Overcoming Irrational Fears and is followed by comments on each of the fear objects listed in the Steps to Freedom in Christ.

Worksheet 1: Overcoming Anxiety

The Greek word for anxiety, *merimna*, is derived from two root words: *merizo* (divide) and *nous* (mind). To be anxious is to be double-minded, and double-minded people are unstable in all their ways (James 1:8). Jesus illustrates this in Matthew 6:24-25, where He explains that we cannot serve two masters. We will love the one and hate the other. He then says, "For this reason I say to you, do not be worried (*merimna*) about your life." The King James translation reads, "Take no thought for your life." We shouldn't have to worry about tomorrow because God cares for the birds and the lilies of the field, and we are worth much more than those. The anecdote for anxiety is to seek first the kingdom of God and His righteousness (verse 33). To cast your anxiety onto Christ (1 Peter 5:6-9), work through the following process.

1. PRAY (PHILIPPIANS 4:6).

> *Dear heavenly Father, I come to You as Your child, purchased by the blood of the Lord Jesus Christ. I declare my dependence on You, and I acknowledge my need for Your wisdom, power, and grace. I know that apart from Christ, I can do nothing. You know the thoughts and intentions of my heart. I feel as though I am double-minded, and I need Your peace to guard my heart and my mind. I humble myself before You and choose to trust You to exalt me at the proper time in any way You choose. I place my trust in You to supply all my needs according to Your riches in glory and to guide me into all truth. I ask for Your divine guidance so that I may fulfill my calling to live a righteous and responsible life by faith*

in the power of the Holy Spirit. "Search me, O God, and know
my heart; try me and know my anxious thoughts; and see if there
be any hurtful way in me, and lead me in the everlasting way"
[Psalm 139:23]. *In Jesus' precious name I pray. Amen.*

2. RESOLVE ANY PERSONAL AND SPIRITUAL CONFLICTS (JAMES 4:7).

The Steps to Freedom in Christ will help you submit to God and resist
the devil. Eliminating the influence of the evil one and seeking a peaceful
sense of God's presence will leave you with a clear and single-focused mind.

3. STATE THE PROBLEM.

A problem well stated is half-solved. When you are anxious, you can't
see the forest for the trees. Put the problem in perspective. Will it matter
for eternity? The process of worrying is likely to take a greater toll on you
than the problem itself will.

4. DISTINGUISH BETWEEN FACTS AND ASSUMPTIONS.

You may be fearful of the facts, but facts won't make you anxious. You
are probably anxious because you don't know what will happen tomorrow. Unfortunately, we not only often make assumptions but also tend to
assume the worst.

5. DETERMINE WHAT YOU HAVE THE RIGHT AND ABILITY TO CONTROL.

You are responsible only for that which you have the right and ability
to control. You are not responsible for that which you shouldn't or can't
control. Your sense of worth is tied only to that for which you are responsible. If you aren't living a responsible life, you *should* feel anxious! Don't
try to cast your own responsibility onto Christ—He will undoubtedly
throw it right back.

6. LIST EVERYTHING YOU CAN DO ABOUT THE SITUATION THAT IS YOUR RESPONSIBILITY AND THEN COMMIT YOURSELF TO DO IT (ISAIAH 32:17).

7. DECLARE THAT THE REST IS GOD'S RESPONSIBILITY.

If you still feel anxious, you are probably assuming responsibilities
that God never intended you to have. Continue living according to Philippians 4:6-9.

Worksheet 2: Overcoming Irrational Fears

1. ANALYZE YOUR FEAR.

Fear is the God-given natural reaction we feel when our physical and psychological safety is threatened. However, irrational fears are developed the same way other flesh patterns are developed. Try to ascertain when the fear became prominent and what was happening in your life at that time. There is always a cause-and-effect relationship. The original cause may be a traumatic experience, or it could be a condemning thought from the enemy. People are not in bondage to traumas; they are in bondage to the lies they believe as a result of traumas. The root of any phobia is a belief that is not based in truth (a lie). These false beliefs must be rooted out and replaced with God's truth. Start by asking for God's guidance.

> *Dear heavenly Father, I come to You as Your child. I put myself under Your protective care and acknowledge that You are the only legitimate fear object in my life. I confess that I have been fearful and anxious because of my belief and lack of trust. I have not always lived by faith in You, and too often I have relied on my own strength and resources. I thank You for forgiving me in Christ. I choose to believe the truth that You have not given me a spirit of fear, but of power, love, and discipline [2 Timothy 1:7]. Therefore, I renounce any spirit of fear. I ask You to reveal to my mind all the fears that have been controlling me. Show me how I have become fearful and the lies I have believed. I desire to live a responsible life in the power of the Holy Spirit. Show me how these fears have kept me from living a responsible life. I ask this so that I can confess, renounce, and overcome every fear by faith in You. In Jesus' name I pray. Amen.*

2. ANALYZE YOUR LIFESTYLE.

How has your fear prevented you from doing what is right and responsible?

How has your fear compelled you to do what is wrong and irresponsible?

How has your fear prompted you to compromise your witness for Christ?

3. PRAYERFULLY WORK OUT A PLAN OF RESPONSIBLE BEHAVIOR.

4. DETERMINE IN ADVANCE WHAT YOUR RESPONSE WILL BE TO ANY FEAR
OBJECT.

5. COMMIT YOURSELF TO CARRY OUT THE PLAN OF ACTION IN THE POWER
OF THE HOLY SPIRIT.

Specific Fears Mentioned in the Steps to Freedom in Christ

Phobias are irrational fears. To overcome them, one needs to discern
irrational beliefs. To be legitimate, a fear object must have two attributes:
It must be imminent and potent. In other words, we must be aware of its
presence and acknowledge that it has some power to damage us physically
or psychologically. God is the ultimate fear object because He is omnipres-
ent and omnipotent. You overcome your irrational fear by removing just
one of the attributes. In many cases, what we fear is inevitable. It may happen, but that doesn't mean we have to fear it or be unduly anxious about
unforeseen events. The following fear objects are taken in order from page
19 in *Steps to Freedom in Christ* (Regal, 2001).

1. FEAR OF DEATH

Physical death is still imminent, but it is no longer potent. "'Death is
swallowed up' in victory. 'O death, where is your victory? O death, where
is your sting?'" (1 Corinthians 15:54-55). The person who is free from the
fear of death is free to live today. The apostle Paul wrote, "For to me, to
live is Christ and to die is gain" (Philippians 1:21). Jesus is the resurrection and the life, and those who believe in Him will live (spiritually) even
if they die (physically) (John 11:25). "[Jesus] partook of [flesh and blood],
that through death He might render powerless him who had the power of
death, that is, the devil, and might free those who through fear of death
were subject to slavery all their lives" (Hebrews 2:14-15). The ultimate
value is our eternal life, which we already have in Christ, and not our physical or natural life, which we will all lose someday.

2. FEAR OF NEVER LOVING OR BEING LOVED

It has been said that people don't commit suicide unless they have
given up all hope for love. That can happen when Christianity becomes an
obligation or a ritual instead of a relationship. The greatest commandment
is to love the Lord our God with all our heart and to love our neighbors as

ourselves. Agape love does not depend on the object. God loves us because He is love, and that is why it is unconditional. God loves all of His children the same, and He would continue to love them just as much even if they failed to live up to certain standards. In such cases God may discipline us, but that just proves His love.

Every Christian has the capacity to love others. We love because He first loved us. People cannot sincerely help others without helping themselves in the process. That is why it is more blessed to give than to receive. Those who are waiting for someone other than God to love them may wait a long time. If you want someone to love you, try loving someone. When we do nothing from selfishness or empty conceit, and with humility of mind regard one another as more important than ourselves, and do not merely look out for our own personal interests, but also the interests of others (Philippians 2:3-4), we are loving and will feel loved.

3. FEAR OF SATAN

The devil is prowling around like a roaring lion, looking for someone to devour (1 Peter 5:8). He may well be successful when people believe he is a greater fear object than God is. Satan wants to be feared because he wants to be worshipped. Fearing Satan more than God elevates Satan as a greater object of worship than God. He gains some measure of control over us when we respond in fear. Such spiritual encounters are imminent but should not be potent because Satan has been disarmed (Colossians 2:15), and every child of God is alive in Christ and seated with Him in heaven (Ephesians 2:6). All authority has been given to Jesus in heaven and on earth (Matthew 28:18). Therefore Satan has no authority over any believer. Every believer has the spiritual authority and power to do God's will, and Satan can't touch us as long as we abide in Christ (1 John 5:18) and put on the armor of God (Ephesians 6:10-17). Satan cannot do anything about our identity and position in Christ except to lie about them, and if he can get us to believe his lies, we will live accordingly—to our detriment.

4. FEAR OF EMBARRASSMENT

This fear often reveals a lack of security in Christ. Secure people have learned to laugh at themselves when they goof up. We will all embarrass ourselves sometime. On the other hand, we shouldn't seek to embarrass ourselves as some do when seeking attention. The basic issue with the fear of embarrassment is often the fear of others. The temptation is to become a man pleaser. The apostle Paul wrote; "For am I now seeking the favor of men, or of God? Or am I striving to please men? If I were still striving to please men, I would not be a bond-servant of Christ" (Galatians 1:10). People pleasers become slaves of other people. We should not fear being "fools for Christ's sake" (1 Corinthians 4:10).

5. Fear of Failure

Fear of failure is far more common than most fears and drives many leaders to burn out. Christians need to accurately define success and failure. Success includes…

- knowing God and His ways (Joshua 1:7-8)

- becoming the person God created you to be (Philippians 3:12-14; 1 Thessalonians 4:3)

- being a good steward of your time, talent, and treasure

That is the path we are all on. If we don't follow those steps in that order, we will not live up to our potential. To stumble and fall is not to fail (Proverbs 24:16). Failure comes when you say, "I was pushed" and then fail to learn from the experience. We will always feel some fear if we are growing, and the only way to overcome the fear of failure is to step out in faith and do the godly thing we fear the most. We learn more from our mistakes than we do from temporal successes.

6. Fear of Being Victimized

We cannot promise people that they will not be victimized. For some believers in this fallen world, victimization is imminent. But we *can* promise them that they don't have to remain victims anymore. And if the victimization leads to death, we can assure them that though they will be absent from the body, they will be at home with the Lord (2 Corinthians 5:8). We are always assured of God's presence, and His sustaining grace will never leave us or forsake us. Suffering is often a part of our sanctification. There are many books and testimonies of people who have not only survived tragedies but even flourished. Often such suffering shapes our lives for greater service.

> We also exult in our tribulations, knowing that tribulation brings about perseverance, and perseverance, proven character; and proven character, hope; and hope does not disappoint, because the love of God has been poured out within our hearts through the Holy Spirit who was given us (Romans 5:3-5).

Trials and tribulations are parts of this worldly life. God will never allow them to destroy us, but they do reveal our character and our level of maturity. "We do not lose heart, but though our outer man is decaying, yet our inner man is being renewed day by day. For momentary, light affliction is producing for us an eternal weight of glory far beyond all comparison" (2 Corinthians 4:16-17). We can get through any trial if we don't lose hope, which is the present assurance of some future good.

7. FEAR OF REJECTION

It is going to happen. We cannot live without experiencing some rejection from others. The fear of rejection is the primary reason why some people don't share their faith. It is an irrational fear that stops us from being witnesses. Denying someone the good news because we may get rejected isn't rational. In many cases, people are not rejecting you; they are rejecting Christ, but you may be the one who takes the brunt of the attack. Hear what the apostle Peter said: "[Come] to Him as to a living stone which has been rejected by men, but is choice and precious in the sight of God" (1 Peter 2:4). Jesus lived the perfect life, and *everyone* rejected Him during His trial. The person who is secure in Christ has the potential to stand alone if need be, but you are actually never alone, because God is always with you.

Reaching out to others always includes some risk because of the possibility of being rejected. But it is a risk worth taking because those who don't make the effort will miss meaningful relationships. "Accept one another, just as Christ also accepted us to the glory of God" (Romans 15:7). Peter addressed this issue squarely.

> Who is there to harm you if you prove zealous for what is good? But even if you should suffer for the sake of righteousness, you are blessed. And do not fear their intimidation, and do not be troubled, but sanctify Christ as Lord in your hearts,

always being ready to make a defense to everyone who asks you to give an account for the hope that is in you, yet with gentleness and reverence; and keep a good conscience so that in the things in which you are slandered, those who revile your good behavior in Christ will be put to shame (1 Peter 3:13-16).

8. FEAR OF MARRIAGE

This fear usually comes with some personal history. People have seen their parents or others suffer through a bad marriage, and they don't want to experience the same. Couple that with a fear of commitment to one person. What if it doesn't work? A life that responds to what-ifs and worst-case scenarios isn't worth living. The pessimist asks, "What are the risks if I do?" The person of faith asks, "How might God use this if I do?" God works primarily in our lives through committed relationships.

Marriage is not a contract that can be broken. It is a covenant relationship that aids in our sanctification if we will stay committed and choose to mature in the Lord. Nobody can keep spouses or parents from being the people God created them to be, and if both spouses keep that focus, the marriage will be a blessing to them. God does allow for divorce in the cases of adultery and abandonment by an unbeliever. The latter is avoided if care has been taken not to be unequally yoked. Should one be unfaithful, however, the remaining spouse can still be the person God created him or her to be. There is life after every failed relationship if we learn from it and continue in our pursuit of being the people God created us to be.

9. FEAR OF DISAPPROVAL

This too is inevitable. Consider Jesus' experience with the Jewish rulers: "Many even of the rulers believed in Him, but because of the Pharisees they were not confessing Him, for fear that they would be put out of the synagogue; for they loved the approval of men rather than the approval of God" (John 12:42).

People feel guilty when they have done something wrong, but they feel shamed when they sense something is wrong with them. There is no guilt and shame for the redeemed. There is no condemnation for those who are in Christ Jesus (Romans 8:1), and there is nothing wrong with you if you are a child of God. Many Christians should stop trying to find out what is wrong with them and focus more on what is right about them now that they are new creations in Christ. That is the only answer for overcoming the shame of feeling as if you're a nobody.

If you want to increase your approval rating, follow the example of those who walked before us in faith. The writer of Hebrews wrote, "Now faith is the assurance of things hoped for, the conviction of things not seen. For by it the men of old gained approval" (Hebrews 11:1-2). The apostle Paul wrote, "Be diligent to present yourself approved to God as a workman who does not need to be ashamed, accurately handling the word of truth" (2 Timothy 2:15).

10. Fear of Divorce

This misplaced focus is not an effective motivation for building a strong marriage. Remember, fear is a powerful motivator for good or evil. Making an effort to avoid divorce does not lead to the same behavior as doing what it takes to make a good marriage. Responding to another person's dissatisfactions will be a never-ending trial. Trying to appease fleshly demands will only deepen the flesh patterns. Expressed dissatisfactions are seldom the same issues that bring satisfaction. Martha was dissatisfied with her sister Mary because she was bothered and worried about so many things, but Mary had chosen the best part (Luke 10:38-42). Fearing divorce has led many people to buy things, take trips, and give in to demands, but those things rarely promote strong marriages. A meaningful relationship is what satisfies. Hungering and thirsting after righteousness is what satisfies. Love and forgiveness are like glue that holds families together.

11. Fear of Becoming or Being Homosexual

Homosexuality is a lie. There are no homosexuals. Of course, people experience homosexual feelings, tendencies, and behaviors, but God created us as males and females. The lie often begins as a result of sexual abuse and tempting thoughts. People who have tempting thoughts toward others of the same sex may start questioning their sexuality. They falsely conclude, *If I am thinking these thoughts, I must be one of them.* If they believe that lie and act on it, they have used their bodies as instruments of unrighteousness and bonded to the other person. The Steps lead these people to renounce that lie, ask God to reveal every sexual use of their bodies as instruments of unrighteousness, and ask God to break that bond emotionally, physically, and spiritually. (See *Winning the Battle Within* for more help.)

12. FEAR OF GOING CRAZY

Often this fear is due to spiritual battles in people's minds. Usually, few people will disclose this hidden burden, but the Steps address this issue as well. People can have neurological problems, and that should be considered if there is no mental peace after submitting to God and resisting the devil. Anxiety disorders are the number one mental health problem throughout the world, followed by depression and anger, which our ministry addresses in the books *Freedom from Fear, Overcoming Depression, Getting Anger Under Control,* and *Overcoming Addictive Behavior.*

Many people drink alcohol and take drugs because they have no mental peace, which only adds to the problem. The answer according to the apostle Paul is to turn to God, dwell on things that are true, pure, and lovely, and then live accordingly (Philippians 4:6-10).

13. FEAR OF FINANCIAL PROBLEMS

Most Christians have been taught that God will supply all their needs according to His riches in glory (Philippians 4:19). So a lack of trust may be the issue, but other issues can precipitate this fear as well. First is contentment. "If we have food and covering, with these we shall be content" (1 Timothy 6:8). Many are not content with what they have, and the love of money (not money itself) is a root of all sorts of evil (verse 10). The apostle Paul says, "Not that I speak from want, for I have learned to be content in whatever circumstances I am" (Philippians 4:11). That is a goal every Christian can and should achieve. Actually, rich people struggle with this fear as much as—and in some cases more than—those who seem to be poor. It is better to be poor in the eyes of this world and rich in the eyes of God.

Second, we should be good stewards of all that God has entrusted to us (1 Corinthians 4:1-3). Life is not an entitlement, it is an entrustment. Poor stewardship can lead to hardship. If we are not assuming our responsibility, we *should* feel anxious.

Third, if a man isn't willing to work, neither should he eat (2 Thessalonians 3:10). "We are His workmanship, created in Christ Jesus for good

works, which God prepared beforehand so that we would walk in them"
(Ephesians 2:10).

14. FEAR OF PAIN AND ILLNESS

Pain and illness are imminent; therefore, we need to learn how to cope
with them. Our outer person is decaying, and regardless of how strong
our faith is, God has not promised that we will all die in perfect health.
Many in the Western world think of pain as an enemy, but it isn't. If we
couldn't feel pain, we would be covered with scars in a matter of weeks.
Where there is no pain, there is no gain. Childbirth is painful, and so is
growing in grace. We learn obedience the same way Jesus did—through
the things we suffer (Hebrews 5:8). God comforts us in all our afflictions,
and we share in His sufferings, which enables us to give comfort to others
(see 2 Corinthians 1:3-6).

15. FEAR OF NEVER GETTING MARRIED

The apostle Paul wrote, "But I say to the unmarried and to widows that
it is good for them if they remain even as I" (1 Corinthians 7:8). Throughout history, the church has viewed celibacy as a gift for some. To remain
single is nobler, but it is not more normal in our culture. There is a lot of
social pressure to get married, and not to do so signifies failure in some
people's eyes, often the parents. Pressure to get married has led some to
make or accept a proposal that ends up far worse than remaining single.

The fear of remaining single can motivate people to do something they
will regret. Being single does not mean a life of loneliness or a sign of rejection. It is better to have no one to marry than to marry the wrong person.
We find our meaning in life by fulfilling our calling, which may mean no
marriage or children for reasons we may not know in this life. Under the
lordship of God, marriage may happen in the course of living, but it is not
something we should try to make happen. We don't try to make things
happen while serving in God's kingdom; rather, things happen as He
directs. But when He opens the door, we should take advantage of every
opportunity to His honor and glory.

16. FEAR OF THE FUTURE

The future is in God's hands. We learn to take one day at a time and
trust God for tomorrow. The key is to live a responsible life each day. Fear

of the future leads to anxiety because we don't know what is going to happen tomorrow. You will feel depressed if you think life is hopeless, but it never is with God. Consider the worst-case scenario, and then ask yourself if you can live with it with God's help. If you say yes, you have nothing to fear.

17. Fear of the Death of a Loved One

This too is inevitable. It helps to have an eternal perspective. "Precious in the sight of the Lord is the death of His godly ones" (Psalm 116:15). That doesn't make sense from a temporal perspective, but it does from an eternal perspective. They are in His presence. We suffer, but not as those who have no hope.

Our reaction to losses is the primary cause for depression (see *Overcoming Depression*). A prolonged depression indicates an unhealthy attachment to people, places, and things we have no right or ability to control. Everything we have in this fallen world is temporal, and someday we will lose it all. Tennessee Williams said, "We are all terrorized by the idea of impermanence." Actually, there is no permanence in this world, there is only change. The apostle James addressed this issue.

> Come now, you who say, "Today or tomorrow we will go to such and such a city, and spend a year there and engage in business and make a profit." Yet you do not know what your life will be like tomorrow. You are just a vapor that appears for a little while and then vanishes away. Instead, you ought to say, "If the Lord wills, we will live and also do this and that" (James 4:13-15).

18. Fear of Confrontation

The fear of being rejected and the fear of failure are probably the basic issues behind this fear. We must have the right attitude before we confront anything or anyone. The purpose is to restore those who have fallen or to stand for the sake of righteousness. Sin will abound if good people do nothing. We stand more to lose in the long run if we tolerate sin and fail to discipline, and discipline should prove our love just as it proves God's. Courage is needed. "The wicked flee when no one is pursuing, but the righteous are bold as a lion" (Proverbs 28:1). Acts 4:31 reads, "When they had prayed, the place where they had gathered together was shaken, and they were all filled with the Holy Spirit and began to speak the word of God with boldness." Remember that the fear of the Lord is the beginning of wisdom.

19. Fear of Being a Hopeless Case

You can live for seven minutes without air, seven days without water, and forty days without food, but you can't live for a moment without hope. No Christian is hopeless when rightly related to God. Mother Teresa gained world renown for helping those the world considered hopeless.

We all want to be the helper, but when we don't allow people to help us, we are robbing them of their opportunity to love. Pride keeps us from receiving love. We think that we don't want to depend on others, but we all are interdependent, and that is how God designed the church. We depend on the gas station for gas, the grocery store for food, and the emergency room for immediate care. We absolutely need God, and we necessarily need each other. God will supply all our needs, but He usually does that through other people.

If you find yourself in a hopeless situation, be a blessing to those who are trying to help and not a complainer, and they will love you even more.

20. Fear of Specific People

We fear certain people only when they are present. The real question is, what power do they have over us? In most cases, the only power they have over us is what we give them. Consider the worst-case scenario. "Do not fear those who kill the body but are unable to kill the soul; but rather fear Him who is able to destroy both soul and body in hell" (Matthew 10:28). Only God has the right to determine who we are, and nobody can keep us from being the people God created us to be.

21. Fear of Losing Our Salvation

Obviously, Calvinists and Arminians disagree on this important issue. Even the best intentioned Christians will choose to sin at some time. Therefore, neither side of the argument believes that sin costs us our salvation. When Christ died for our sins, they were in the future.

God's gracious love and acceptance do not give us a license to sin but rather empower us so we don't have to sin.

We are not forgiven when we confess our sins; we are forgiven when we put our trust in Jesus, because He died on the cross for our sins. Confession simply means to agree with God. Confession is essentially the same issue as walking in the light, as described in 1 John 1:9. It means to live in constant moral agreement with God, and we can always do that because we are already forgiven the moment we are born again.

The issue is more a question of God's sovereignty and our responsibility. Did we come to Christ primarily because of God's decision or because of our own decisions? If the choice was primarily our own, the Arminians would argue that we can subsequently choose to reject Christ and forfeit our salvation. That would seem to make the choice for salvation depend on us more than on God. Calvinists would point to Jesus' statement, "No one can come to Me unless the Father who sent Me draws him; and I will raise him up on the last day" (John 6:44). But this logically leads to a limited atonement, which is hard to defend when Scripture teaches that "whoever will call on the name of the Lord will be saved" (Romans 10:13). Most people would agree that double election is not taught in Scripture. Some may be elected to be saved, but no one is elected to be lost. A sign above the door to eternal life invites all to come to Jesus. As you step into the kingdom of God and look back, you will see a sign that says you were known from eternity past.

The question is not so much whether we will hold on to God but rather whether He will let go of us, and that question is easy to answer. Jesus said, "My sheep hear My voice, and I know them, and they follow Me; and I give eternal life to them, and they will never perish; and no one will snatch them out of My hand" (John 10:27-28). The apostle Paul wrote, "Having also believed, you were sealed in Him with the Holy Spirit of promise, who is given as a pledge of our inheritance, with a view to the redemption of God's own possession, to the praise of His glory" (Ephesians 1:13-14).

Some will choose to walk away from God, but the apostle John wrote, "They went out from us, but they were not really of us; for if they had been of us, they would have remained with us; but they went out, so that it would be shown that they all are not of us" (1 John 2:19). "Once saved always saved" is not a good way to express our security in Christ. That would open the door for us to go on sinning so that grace may abound, which is precisely what the apostle Paul wrote against in Romans 6.

Many Christians question their salvation when they are struggling with sin. But in fact, they have it backward. They should question their salvation if sinning *didn't* bother them. But if it is bothering them, that is pretty good proof that the Holy Spirit is in residence. Finally, both good Calvinists and good Arminians believe that we can and should feel secure in Christ.

22. FEAR OF NOT BEING LOVED BY GOD

Many Christians question God's love even though "God demonstrates His own love toward us, in that while we were yet sinners, Christ died for us" (Romans 5:8). If God loved us before we were His children, wouldn't He love us still? God loves us because it is His nature to love us. Agape love does not depend on the object. "We have come to know and have believed the love which God has for us. God is love, and the one who abides in love abides in God, and God abides in him" (1 John 4:16). To question God's love is to question His character. To say, "I don't see how God could love me" (or someone else) is to equate our capacity to love with His.

23. FEAR OF HAVING COMMITTED THE UNPARDONABLE SIN

The passage in question is Matthew 12:31-32:

> Therefore I say to you, any sin and blasphemy shall be forgiven people, but blasphemy against the Spirit shall not be forgiven. Whoever speaks a word against the Son of Man, it shall be forgiven him; but whoever speaks against the Holy Spirit, it shall not be forgiven him, either in this age, or in the age to come.

Just prior to this statement, Jesus had responded to the Pharisees' accusation that He performed miracles by the power of Beelzebul, a ruling territorial spirit. In response, Jesus said that if He were casting out demons by the power of Beelzebul, Satan would be casting out Satan. Satan would be divided against himself, and his kingdom could not stand. Jesus then explained that because He was casting out demons by the Spirit of God, the kingdom of God had come upon them (Matthew 12:28). Clearly, they were rejecting the Spirit of God by crediting His work to Beelzebul.

So why did Jesus say that a person can speak against Him but not against the Holy Spirit? The unique role of the Holy Spirit was and is to give evidence to the work of Christ and to lead us into all truth (see John 14:17-19; 16:7-15). The only unpardonable sin is the sin of unbelief. If we reject the testimony given to us by the Holy Spirit, fight off His conviction of our sin, and never accept the truth, we will never come to Christ for salvation. In Christ, all our sins are forgiven. Therefore, no Christian can commit the unpardonable sin. Only an unregenerate person who refuses to come to Christ will die in his or her sins. The accuser of the brethren, however, will often try to convince Christians that they have committed the unpardonable sin so they will live in defeat.

Christians, however, *can* quench the Spirit. If we do, we will impede the work of God and live a less than victorious life, but we will not lose our salvation.

NOTES

Introduction

1. See my book *Discipleship Counseling* (Regal Books, 2004).

2. I expand upon this much more in my book *The Core of Christianity* (Harvest House, 2009).

3. See my book *The Steps to Freedom in Christ* (Gospel Light, 2004), available in bookstores, online, or directly from Freedom in Christ Ministries. The Steps connect inquirers directly to God through prayer and help them to resolve their personal and spiritual conflicts.

4. Edmund J. Bourne, *Healing Fear* (Oakland, CA: New Harbinger, 1998), 2.

5. Bourne, *Healing Fear*, 5.

Chapter 8—Ministering Freedom to the Hispanic Church

1. Corporate conflict resolution is explained in Neil Anderson, *Extreme Church Makeover* (Ventura, CA: Regal Books, 2005).

MORE GREAT HARVEST HOUSE BOOKS BY NEIL ANDERSON

The Bondage Breaker®
Overcoming Negative Thoughts,
Irrational Feelings, and Habitual Sins

The Bondage Breaker® Study Guide

The Bondage Breaker® Youth Edition
(Neil Anderson and Dave Park)

The Core of Christianity
Rediscovering Authentic Unity and
Personal Wholeness in Christ

Winning the Battle Within
Realistic Steps to Overcoming Sexual Strongholds

Getting Anger Under Control
Overcoming Unresolved Resentment,
Overwhelming Emotions, and the Lies Behind Anger
(Neil Anderson and Rich Miller)

Daily in Christ
(Neil Anderson and Joanne Anderson)

Freedom from Fear
(Neil Anderson and Rich Miller)

Winning Spiritual Warfare

Praying by the Power of the Spirit

Breaking the Bondage of Legalism
When Trying Harder Isn't Enough
(Neil Anderson, Rich Miller, and Paul Travis)